BUZZING!

Tales of empathy and optimism

For Alex & Terry

First published 2023 by The Modern Agency
Copyright © Peter Cordwell 2023

The right of Peter Cordwell to be identified as the author of this work has been asserted by him in accordance with the Copyright, Designs and Patents Act 1988.

Illustrations by Dean Ford ©2023
Cover design by Dean Ford and The Modern Agency ©2023

Set in 11pt Plantin MT Pro

All rights reserved. No part of this publication may be reproduced, stored in or introduced into a retrieval system, or transmitted, in any form, or by any means (electronic, mechanical, photocopying, recording or otherwise) without the prior written permission of the publisher. Any person who does any unauthorised act in relation to this publication may be liable to criminal prosecution and civil claims for damages.

Introduction

THESE short stories were written mostly during Covid as an escape to the 'office' upstairs from the clutches of the pandemic.

Almost all of them started with a thought from the past, a character or a situation. I just bashed away on my ancient Apple Mac until I got some kind of twist in the tale.

After four or five stories I realised they were all light and positive, and how I had no time at all for the 'dark' that many people seem to prefer these days.

All the scenarios are fictitious but I've used two or three names from the distant past. I hope, in particular, that Christopher Hadley is alive and well, and won't mind at all. Google bore no fruit.

During this time of polarised love and the other thing, I hope the stories make you feel a little bit better in yourself.

Contents

1	Saving Mike the Postman
2	Young James on the ball
3	The artist who went for the coffees
4	Until one of us pegs it
5	Bumping into Christopher Hadley
6	The sky blue suit
7	The tears of Penelope Coomber
8	Something's cooking for Simon
9	The twigs of democracy
10	The Orange Menace
11	The 'lino' and the star player
12	Postcode problems
13	Ring them bells
14	Leaving Tom to Tom
15	God's great sense of humour
16	Young Mr Dexter and shy Miss Bright
17	Jamal's final performance
18	Winston's change of pace
19	The local sprinter
20	2084

Saving Mike the Postman

IT was one of those seaside towns dying on its feet on the Kent coast in the 1980s, boarded-up windows the opening evidence for the prosecution. Even the tide didn't want to come in.

The local Gazette reflected it all, down from 12 broadsheet pages to eight as the local population stayed more or less the same between June and August.

There seemed to be no way out of the gloom. But suddenly, amazingly, there was...

The Gazette's chief reporter, their only reporter really, had recently done a moonlight, and his ancient, improbable replacement turned out to be a saviour on two fronts, the paper and the sea.

Even more unlikely as the catalyst to happier times was someone whose last name, as far as everyone seemed to think, was The Postman. Mike the Postman.

The new reporter, relaxing somewhere in his mid-to-late-sixties, had an odd name too – Sidney Carson. But that's quickly explained. His father had been a

Dickens nut and loved A Tale of Two Cities in particular. Sidney – don't ask me why he didn't spell it Sydney – recalled chuckling to himself when reading the novel as a young man and wondering what life-saving antics of the lead character would find their way into his own life. The antics took their time but, it could be said, achieved something similar, give or take a guillotine.

Sidney was retired (as he thought) to a neat and shaded one-bedroom flat 200 yards or so up from the front. Perhaps Dickens' much-quoted love of the Kent coast had something to do with it psychologically. CD: 'You cannot think how delightful and fresh the place is – and how good the walks.'

Sidney – never 'Sid' for some reason – was a local paper natural, dapper with the ever-present smile behind a thousand stories. He saw the ad for a 'Chief Reporter' as he passed The Gazette window and couldn't help but walk in, beaming.

The editor, Paul Page – talk about born to byline! – snapped him up by virtue of a readily accepted minimum wage and miniscule exes, it being easy, Mr Page pointed out with some embarrassment, to walk to almost everywhere in town.

Sidney didn't mind. Selling up in London had left him enough to see out his days frugally, and doing the job he loved in sea air made perfect sense.

Paul Page shared a cubby hole of an office – Underwood typewriter to Underwood typewriter - with the sports editor, Harold Desmond. But the Gazette was kept going – they both admitted, if only to themselves - by the two advertising ladies, Janet Strong and Charity Ball, the latter who would be described these days as black and bubbly.

And Sidney himself soon a boon. Every day he would wend his way down to Josie's Café by 8am for tea and two toast. After a while anyone with a story – from a potentially dangerous crossing to a new folk singing duo – knew they'd see him there; knew he'd interview them; knew he'd take pictures with his funny little Pentax camera.

Custom at the cafe was boosted to such an extent over Sidney's first six weeks that Josie, the Cockney owner with her husband, Reggie, served tea and two toast on the house.

Almost everyone got in the habit of calling out good morning to Sidney because Sidney always called out good morning to them, even if they were on the other side of the road. Sidney never missed a single soul because he knew that everyone, literally, was a "contact" and therefore a possible story.

What he didn't know was how it would all lead to the Gazette's biggest-ever campaigning story.

Janet and Charity gamely chased ads day after day. Five estate agents were down to three but at least regular. It was harder work with the shops and restaurants on the front, including the one betting shop that only came alive during the Cheltenham and Royal Ascot festivals.

Half a dozen struggling B&B's and a health centre only had the dosh to advertise once a month, and the big but sad old Seaview Hotel, which had held conferences and various musical events in its heyday, was more or less keeping its head down and hoping.

Births, deaths, marriages and lonely hearts brought in a few pounds every week, but most welcome by far was the incongruous but life-saving four-page wrap-around advert every four to six weeks...four great, six a bit nervy.

The "wrap" came from a rich but presumably dense young property developer based in London called Stuart Sharpe, still not 30. Word had it that Stuart's father Donald had the fondest childhood memories of staying at the Seaview Hotel and more or less ordered his son to do business in the area.

The unspoken prayer at the Gazette was: Please God, don't ever let Donald die…

It was Janet who noticed that business was slowly but perceptively picking up following Sidney's arrival, and it was Charity who worked out why. Together they told Paul Page at their weekly meeting: "What it is, PP, he pops in so many places and sees so many people – lots of them in Josie's Café – and finds a reason, an angle, to give them a write-up, big or small. He's a magnet. The result is that a quarter of them or more take out an ad as well. The man's a life saver.'

Janet added the story of the flower shop. 'It's run by Mrs Misery,' she said, 'but Sidney got her eating out of his hand on his first visit and she took out an ad the following day. Okay, mostly wreaths, but nevertheless…I reckon she's got other ideas for young Sidney.'

After the slump they'd been through, Paul and Harold instinctively ducked under the beams of optimism that Sidney had brought with him as he bashed out his multiple stories late in the afternoon. But both agreed after a month or two that they too sensed something in the air.

That something turned out to be a someone, Mike the Postman.

Among the many people Sidney hailed in the streets most mornings was cheerful Mike. He was in his early forties and unmarried. It was assumed, sometimes unkindly, that he'd never had a girlfriend. He was shy and had a slight stutter. He found it difficult to look people in the eye. The era was approaching when individuals like Mike might be said to have 'special needs'. Perhaps he had what's now known as Asperger's.

But, in truth, he had no 'needs' or problems at all. He loved his long-term job and the town loved Mike. That's all he needed. He delivered the post come rain, snow or shine. He was more reliable than the town hall clock, and Sidney mused that he and Mike did in fact have a lot in common. The job was the thing. The job was everything.

The job was a kind of salvation.

Yet here was Mike on this particular morning, head down and clearly in the dumps. 'You okay, Mike?' asked Sidney.

'N'no, not really,' said Mike. 'I'I've been sacked. I've got to the end of the month.'

'Sacked?' said Sidney. 'That's not possible.' It was then that he realised he hadn't actually seen Mike for a good few days, a week or more.

'I, er, ah, had 10 days off with asthma after my Mum died,' said Mike. 'I couldn't breathe very well, Mr Carson, but they said it wasn't asthma. They called my doctor to check, and then they sacked me. They said the doctor said I'd never had asthma in my life and nor had anyone in my family.'

Sidney got it straight away. The poor man had had panic attacks after the death of his Mum but had no idea what they were. He looked down at the ground, then exclaimed: "We're not having this, Mike! Are you working tomorrow?'

'Y'yes.'

'Right, I'll join you at the start of your round and we'll get quotes and pictures from EVERY home you visit! Sack our Mike? Never!'

With that, Sidney went without his free tea and two toast and hightailed it to the office, where the instant reaction from Paul, Harold, Janet and Charity was the same as Sidney's: 'Sack our Mike? Never!'

The following day Sidney accompanied Mike on his morning round and, true to form, got pictures and quotes enough to fill all eight of Paul Page's pages. The 100 per cent response backed up the chosen slogan: 'Sack our Mike? Never!'

Back in the office, Sidney got out his shorthand notebook and dialled the Royal Mail in London. He said he had a press inquiry but was told that the Royal Mail didn't take press inquiries of that kind from a local paper, only the nationals. They were far too busy. Send a fax.

'Well, you'll take this one in a few days if you know what's good for you,' said Sidney in rare high dudgeon, slamming the phone down.

Watched intently by the others, as Harold made the tea, Sidney furiously banged out the front page story – turned to Pages 2 and 3 – with quotes and pictures galore from irate residents who were also Royal Mail customers. Paul Page's two-deck splash headline in 96pt Helvetica Bold – alongside Sidney's heart-rending picture of Mike the Postman, read:

Sack our Mike?
NEVER!

As well as urging readers to swamp the Royal Mail switchboard with complaints about Mike's dismissal, Sidney wrote that there would be a protest demonstration in the square outside the town's post office, by the clocktower, on Saturday at 12pm. High Noon, he called it.

On the day in question, a sunny one with a cooling breeze in solidarity, the square was totally packed with people chanting: 'Sack our Mike? Never! Sack our Mike? Never!'

They included all of Mike's workmates, two of whom carried the reluctant postman on their shoulders. The only townspeople not there, it was said, were the families who promised to produce home-made posters for every window and every lamp-post in support of Mike the Postman.

One surprise but very welcome supporter was young moneybags Stuart Sharpe. He'd heard about it after calling Janet on Friday morning about his forthcoming "wrap" – bless him – and motored straight down the M2.

'This place is absolutely buzzing!' he said to Paul Page as he joined the crowd surrounding the clocktower.

'It's always like this for one reason or another,' lied Paul Page, thinking of future wraps and any other business young Stuart might send his way. Then, playing editor, he said: 'Sorry, gotta dash, Stu! Gotta get all this in the next edition!'

With that Paul shook Stuart's hand theatrically and rushed off like an ageing Woodward or Bernstein to join Sidney and the others in the office, which itself was full of people who wanted to add their invaluable two penn'orth to the big story.

Sidney missed no one out. 'Someone's name against someone's quote is the lifeblood of local journalism!' he called out above the fray. 'That and passionate head and shoulders pics!'

People laughed and cheered, as if in an Ealing Studios film, and that evening Paul Page and Co. were clapped into the main bar at the Seaview, which hadn't seen such numbers in five years or more. Stuart Sharpe – 'Stu' to everyone by the end of the day – had stayed and bought drinks all round, and was invited to join the Gazette crew at the table for 10 reserved by Sidney Carson at the big bay window with the, er, well, sea view.

The jubilant mood of the day had quietened down to let in serious discussion, and it was the newly invigorated Paul Page who put their thoughts into words:

'That was great, this is great, we've got another great front page to come next Thursday! But what next? How can we actually win this one? How can we get Mike his job back?'

By the end of the evening, without anyone actually voicing it, the mood was almost sombre. Everyone knew that Royal Mail would probably just ignore the Gazette and its readers. The usual tactic of big business: it would soon be old news.

On the Thursday, Sidney trotted down to Josie's Café as usual and found an almost-packed café reading his story about Mike in the Gazette, each with their own paper, which was good for sales.

He picked up his usual quota of new stories, including one that saw him slip off to the gents to wipe a tear from his eye. Mrs Jenkins' daughter, Gillian, expected twin boys and was thinking of calling them Mike and Sidney. The reporter said that Paul Page would have to write that one up, citing conflict of interest.

The clientele thinned out as people went home or to work. Josie poured herself a cup of tea and joined Sidney at his favourite table by Van Gogh's painting of the Café Terrace at Night.

They chatted away as Sidney nibbled at his toast. The conversation was amiable, as ever, but was going nowhere until Josie said: 'What about his medal?'

'Medal? What medal?' asked Sidney. 'Whose medal?

'Mike's,' said Josie.

'Sorry, I don't know what you're talking about, Josie,' said Sidney, but already feeling the excitement racing up his reporter's spine.

'Oh,' said Josie. 'About seven or eight years ago it must have been, Mike was awarded the Royal Mail's Local Hero medal. Two young thugs tried to take his postbag from him but he held on for dear life. They knocked him about a bit, gave him a bruised face and a black eye, but he wouldn't give them the sack. Sounds a bit ironic now, doesn't it?'

It sounded more than ironic to Sidney, who was already on his feet. He leant forward, grabbed Josie's face by the cheeks and kissed her on the forehead. Then, blushing, dashed out.

At the office, he gathered everyone around and gabbled what Josie had told him. Everyone had forgotten about the Local Hero story – even though it made Page 5 with a picture. Everyone took Mike for granted. The Gazette took Mike for granted. Even Mike took Mike for granted!

Paul took Sidney to the small dusty stockroom where the Gazette's back issues were kept and within minutes they were gazing at the story and the picture, Mike lovingly holding his postbag like a new-born baby.

Sidney snapped the page with his Pentax and within the hour he was calling the Royal Mail about their own Local Hero, threatening television, radio and the Prime Minister as supporters. And yes, he'd fax the photo of the story.

Within another 30 minutes, Mike the Postman had his job back.

For the third week running, the Gazette had Mike on their front page, this time a full page picture of him smiling shyly, surrounded by his cheering, jubilant supporters.

Paul Page excelled himself with a one-word headline in 120pt Helvetica Bold:

SORTED!

Young James on the ball

EIGHT-year-old James was one of those bright, chirpy little kids – bordering on cheeky – that you could never get angry with.

You wouldn't describe him as particularly intelligent but could picture him doing well in life by virtue of his innate energy and enthusiasm.

His teacher, Mrs Herbert, definitely thought so and avoided getting serious with James for fear of her smiling or even having to chuckle in front of the other children. Truth was, she'd grown to love that kind of kid over the years.

The boy was very good at PE and sport, particularly football, and a discussion popped up in the staffroom about whether James should be picked for the primary school team at such a tender age.

Mr Gallier, the PE teacher who also managed the school team, wanted to include him in the squad of what were mostly fourth year boys in those days, 10 and 11-year-olds. Second year James played for an Essex Sunday League Under 9 team, Manor Park Rovers, and scored goals in that age group literally every week. There was no stopping him.

'Yes, but we have to be very aware of child protection,' said Mr Klee, the headteacher, using a phrase that would become so familiar 60 or 70 years later. 'If James was injured playing against 11-year-olds, which is the age of most players towards the end of the season, we would have a case to answer.'

This was October, 1948, and James would be nine in a few months' time. Mr Gallier would get away with playing a nine-year-old in the school team, but eight? James was small for his age as well, not one of those bigger eight-year-olds who also tend to look older.

Mrs Herbert, sipping her tea, added her two penn'orth. 'James plays with the fourth years in the playground, on concrete, and already looks one of the best players.' she said. 'He takes the occasional tumble but gets up straight away. He's a tough little lad...loves his football. He'll be nine in February, but I can't see why he can't be in the school squad now as a substitute for the experience he'd gain.

'And if he had to go on for the last five minutes or so, I'm sure it wouldn't do him any harm.'

Which was the perfect cue for Mr Gallier, fairly new at the school, to exhibit his coaching knowledge to Mr Klee. 'The thing about young James,' he said with studied enthusiasm, 'is that he's so fast, or perhaps quick is a better word. He wouldn't beat any fourth year over 100 yards, or even 50, but none of them would beat him over five or 10. That's obviously why he scores so many goals at Under 9 level. That and his balance, centre of gravity... and his left foot.'

Mr Gallier, obviously pleased with himself, had set up the chance – a definite 'assist' – for Mr Klee to ask about the relevance of James's left foot.

'Well,' said Mr Gallier, approaching full stride, 'being predominantly left-footed is an advantage because right-footed players just can't understand it, or do anything about it. They are thrown by the angles involved and feel uncomfortable facing left-footed players, especially when they are as quick and skilful as young James. It's all about the angles.'

Mr Klee looked far from convinced and Mrs Herbert, smiling to herself, had another sip of tea. None of them could turn to the example, so many years later, of brilliant left-footers like Maradona and Messi bewildering opponents.

Nothing concrete was decided but Mr Gallier reckoned that Mrs Herbert's compromise, not exactly knocked down by Mr Klee, was workable. Dunking a biscuit, he smiled at the thought.

He left it a week or two before actually picking James, just to be on the safe side. He also made a point of finding out where James's team was playing the following Sunday and went along to watch without being spotted, black woolly hat, gloves, glasses and dark green overcoat doing the job well enough. Or so he thought.

As well as seeing James score two more goals, one after a dazzling dribble past two players inside the penalty area, Mr Gallier spotted the PE teacher from the other local primary school who was known to scout for West Ham United – something he would love to do himself – standing next to James's parents on the touchline.

That made up his mind. James would be in the school team squad as a substitute the following Saturday morning, and the chances were that he would play more than just five minutes towards the end of the match.

The boy's father was a tube driver but had Mondays off and usually picked James up from school on that day. Mr Gallier took the chance to say that he was 'thinking' about including James in the school team on the following Saturday.

'Why not?' said James's dad with the same kind of chirpy confidence of his son. 'I don't think it would be too much for him and I know he'd be well excited. He loves his football and so do I. I used to play a bit myself.'

Mr Gallier grinned and mentioned in passing that he'd heard that some pro clubs had already taken an interest in young James.

'Yes,' said his dad, 'but I don't want him getting caught up in all that nonsense at such a young age. It can go to their heads, you know, and parents love to say that their kids have signed for Arsenal or Spurs, some as young as seven! Me and his Mum are not having any of that.'

Mr Gallier agreed but had no compunction about playing an eight-year-old against 11-year-olds. He shared the boy's excitement on the Saturday morning at the local rec. It was a chilly morning but both were positively aglow, and substitute James made his debut not five minutes from time but soon after half time after another lad had taken a knock.

The close game remained goalless until five minutes from time when young James zipped on to a through ball in the area and clipped the ball past the outrushing goalkeeper. The winning goal – and that left foot again.

Among those delighted on the line was the West Ham scout, who patted James's dad on the back. He also gave Mr Gallier a knowing look and wondered out loud if he'd seen him at the local league game the previous Sunday.

'No, not me,' said Mr Gallier with the same kind of smile, but blushing slightly. 'Most Sunday mornings in the garden for me, I'm afraid, attacking dandelions.'

James's goal and exciting performance was reported back to Mr Klee, who included it in his words at the school assembly on Monday morning. James sat there and beamed. So did Mrs Herbert.

The next few years went by in a whirl for young James. Pro club scouts watched 'the boy James' – who was 'a bit special' – at every game he played.

Surprising no one who liked to recall seeing him in the Essex youth football world, he went on to star for Tottenham Hotspurs after first signing professional as a youth player for Chelsea in 1957.

The player, still smallish but even quicker and more skilful, made one point to the six or seven people present on the big day: 'Just one thing,' he said. 'Can everyone stop calling me James. I'm not James, I'm Jimmy. I'm Jimmy Greaves.'

The artist who went for the coffees

LATE one Friday, with almost everybody long gone, I went to turn off the lights and discovered Old Dan, of all people, sketching by the big window.

He tried to shuffle the unwieldy A3 page from the vacated desk without me seeing. Too late, mate. A3's not A4 and the half glimpse I caught was more than enough. Old Dan was an artist! Old Dan, the odd job man. The man who went for the coffees.

We produced magazines, down from six to four thanks to the bankers. Staff of 12 from 18. I oversaw the monthly Creatives. Content, all the usual lifestyle guff.

Old Dan said he had to rush, but this former Fleet Street hack had got a sniff and Dan was rushing nowhere. Still he tried to escape. This was no false modesty. I said: 'Sorry, Dan, but that looks really good to me. Where is it?'

'Primrose Hill,' he said, getting up and looking at everything but me.

I knew I'd talk him round, like a media mongrel does. 'Dan,' I said slowly, 'we'll keep it a total secret between ourselves, tell no one else. Honest, mate. Not a soul.' Old Dan showed me the whole sketch and it was twice as good as the half I'd spotted. I'd worked with lots of illustrators down the years and Old Dan could get in the same lift as all of them.

My head, as ever, was abuzz with an idea, but first I had to ask him: 'Er, how many more have you got, Dan, if you don't mind me asking?"

"Must be nearly 200. Paintings too. Water colours mostly."

About 200? Paintings? I had to sit down. 'I've got an idea, Dan,' I said. 'No pressure, really, but our monthly magazine, Creatives, is going through a bad patch at the moment and I think your work, if the rest is as good as this, could be the boost it needs, a shot in the arm... much-needed oxygen.'

I was overdoing it.

Dan put up more resistance, but it could have been Jose parking his bus against Pep the traffic warden.

Two days later I went for a coffee with Jim Fotherby, the group editor, and told him I'd discovered this amazing artist whose work would grace any magazine. I showed him half a dozen paintings I'd photographed that same night at Dan's flat in Peckham. I'm quick like that.

Jim looked at them, then back at me, then back at them.

He said: 'Go for it. You do the words.' Jim loved playing editors. He agreed on my choice of pseudonym, Caravannio. I really liked Dan Goff but we both reckoned it was too close to home and we genuinely didn't want to expose old Dan.

This was March, 2007, and Old Dan's work went down a storm in Creatives. People loved it and wrote in, asking who Caravannio was. Jim even had the first page framed on his wall and the local radio station had me on to talk about the artist who had become a bit of a mini sensation. I kept mum about Dan and his background, of course; said he was someone I met in a pub one boozy night.

A year later came the crash. Four mags went down to two – Creatives somehow surviving – and Jim called me in to tell me the staff he had to let go. Love that, don't you, let go?

'We'll have to say goodbye to Old Dan as well,' he said. 'Things are that tight. We'll have to keep the place tidy and get our own coffees.'

I looked him in the eye and said: 'I don't think so, Jim.'

'No? Why not?' he said, switching from mate to manager, the way they do.

'Because of this,' I said, showing him the next three pastel drawings for the Caravannio page

'You mean...?' said Jim.

'Yes,' I said, 'but best to keep it to ourselves.'

Until one of us pegs it

JOHN and John were the same age too, 63.

Some had them down automatically as the best of enemies, one John a Millwall fan, the other Charlton Athletic. But any early traces of animosity were swamped by the great passion they shared... for Cribbage.

They worked for an engineering firm at Erith in Kent, hardly the prettiest part of the Garden of England, but their daily games of Crib more than made up for the infamous gloom of the locality.

One of the Johns obviously had to become Jack – as do many a Robinson – to make things easier all round. They tossed for it, the Charlton Athletic John becoming 'Jack'. The other John remained John and much preferred it that way.

The other 27 members of staff went to various cafes and pubs at lunchtime, but John (the Millwall fan) and Jack joined the Crib board they placed in the cosy little room just off reception to play the great little card game, fuelled only by tea and sandwiches.

After a short while John and Jack – remember who's whom? – kept their football comments to the barest minimum. And anyway their tribal disagreements could be reduced to just one word in both cases. Charlton? John: 'Fairies.' Millwall? Jack: 'Thugs.'

If love conquers all, that's what cribbage did for John and Jack. They were both good, fast players. Some other players, who are not so good and fast, announce defensively that's 'it's all down to the cards!' Of course it is. All card games are down to the bloody cards. Or they wouldn't be card games! But knowing what to keep, what to put in your opponent's box (the crib) and how to peg cleverly makes the vital difference between a good player and an ordinary one over the best of, say, 15 games.

And if you play the best of 15, or 51 for that matter, it makes perfect sense to conclude that nous plays a vital part, and the close games are invariably the deciders, the ones that make the big difference.

You can 'lose by a street' – the length of the crib board – or 'die in the hole', reach 120 points, only to watch in horror as your opponent flashes by to 121 points or more, by virtue of his/her 'first take'. Those games, plus typical games won or lost by, say, five to 15 points, make Crib the great little game it is.

You don't need to understand it all (learn the game, by all means!) to appreciate how enjoyable it is for players who are well matched, as in poker and most individual sports. You share something, sometimes for a lifetime.

It's okay to chat during a game, as each player takes turns in shuffling and dealing – 'I should never have doubled that queen' – but, in John and Jack's case, the talk is never about Charlton or Millwall. It could ruin it all, threaten something becoming really special in their lives.

After two years of matches, during which each player opened up leads of 10 to 15 games – occasionally they played after work for an hour or two in The Ship pub in West Street, Erith – the score was 352-338 to John who was John, the Millwall fan.

They weren't born on the same day, thank goodness, but decided to retire together after two years at Erith Engineers. Most of their colleagues found it odd that they should spend so much time together but still came up with a great idea for their joint retirement gift, a very posh Crib board set in dark wood by the name of Italfam, knowing their obsession with the game would continue where they lived, not far apart in SE London.

John who was John lived in Lewisham, closer to Millwall's Den in those days. John who was Jack had a flat in Lee that was handier for Charlton's home ground, The Valley. Neither drove a car but buses and trains were fine. They played almost as often, including evening games over drinks and most weekends.

They were well matched and, very important, it was all totally sporting. No diving or shirt-pulling here, no 'taking one for the team'. If either player counted seven instead of eight, the other would point it out. This could happen over 'One for his nob' for example, the relevant Jack (a Jack who was Jack; joke) cut from the pack... and for want of a nicer phrase.

They enjoyed a drink and sometimes a take-away curry with the evening games, although John who was John had to stick to dry white wine – hardly a Millwall drink - because he'd suffered for the past six or seven years from type two diabetes. 'Dry white' was supposed to be better for him than other forms of alcohol, but he'd mentioned needing an oxygen chamber on a couple of occasions in the past, which began to concern John who was Jack.

And so they played on, playing up and playing the game, as they say. John who was Jack, the Charlton fan, cut the deficit to six over the next three months, 407-401, and reckoned out loud he was 'in the groove'. What neither dared mention was that through Crib and its global sporting reputation – the Americans are mad about the game – they were now the best of friends, football or no football.

Jack was divorced but still saw his two grown-up kids from time to time. John's wife had died four years earlier from breast cancer and he admitted to himself how much Crib and Jack meant to him these days. John was never that well himself but felt a whole lot better after 15 two, 15 four and three's seven, his favourite box score, 'even better than eight!' he liked to repeat to Jack's amusement.

They were even at the point where they could introduce a bizarre prize for the end of their marathon 'never-ending' match, an outlandish 'best of' finale. 'Let's play until one of us pegs it,' said John who was John. 'And let's put £500 each aside for the charity chosen by Millwall or Charlton.'

'Or by Charlton or Millwall,' said John who was Jack.

'Agreed!' grinned John who was still John.

Eight months later, in the middle of the next season, the two Johns faced the football fixture that always impeded their own championship, the local derby at The Den on the Saturday. No way could they play on Saturday or Sunday night, with emotions shredded, and even Monday might be too soon after a debacle for one fan or the other.

Playing Crib the Friday night before the game was the obvious solution, both players agreeing beforehand not to mention the match during the game. One thing they did agree on – one in passing, the other conceding

– was that Millwall always won these games at The Den. You can't argue with the facts.

The Friday came, it was Jack's turn to play at home, just three games adrift of his best mate in their exciting clash of skill and concentration. But John who was John never turned up and wouldn't turn up again. And John who was Jack never went to the game the following day, the first one he'd missed in 20 years.

The £1,000 went a few weeks later to a children's hospice presented gratefully and with some emotion by Mick McCarthy, the Millwall manager, and his team. John who was Jack sat quietly at the back, reflecting on John's idea and holding the Italfam board that meant so much to both of them.

Bumping into Christopher Hadley

OF all the people to bump into totally out of the blue, Christopher Hadley would have been up there, even though it had been all of 15 years.

We'd been in the same fourth year class at primary school, as it was in those days, so at the Watford Gap Services we must have both been 26-ish. One immediately funny thing was that I even remembered the date of his birthday, October the 29th. Mine was November the 19th, so he'd always be those 19 – sorry, 21 – days older than me.

I must have had that memory as part of the effect that Christopher had on me.

At school he was very clever, easily the cleverest boy in Mr Bloomfield's class. We weren't big mates as such. I was more into football and cricket than English and arithmetic, but I was certainly fascinated by him and his cleverness.

Part of it was the way he was with it. He was no boastful clever clogs. There was just a calm authority about Christopher Hadley, a kind of wisdom. His gentle smile was something else as well, and when he was saying something to a small group of us, myself mostly on the outside of things, he seemed to make a perfect kind of sense, his childhood words flowing all around us somehow.

I know it sounds really silly but I can even remember wondering, as he spoke during those dreamlike moments, if he was so much wiser than me because of those 21 days between us. It seemed like 21 years.

So here we both were stopping for a coffee, him heading back to London somewhere and me heading north to see someone in the family.

I saw him first, coming into the Costa area. I'm normally hopeless with names but great with faces. In this case it was both. He sat down three or four tables from me and actually looked in my direction without any signs of recognition on his part.

He was about five feet eight or nine, which made sense, and he had the same slightly egg-shaped Benedict Cumberbatch type of face; smart, clean-shaven and a small briefcase placed to his right at the table for two. He sipped his coffee and opened a novel.

I've never been slow at diving into situations. Why should we be? What's the problem? So, after a couple of minutes, I sauntered over, excused myself and asked if he was Christopher Hadley. He smiled in that same friendly fashion and said he certainly was.

It was okay for me to sit down and rabbit on about how great it was to see him, about how we hadn't been big mates but how I'd always liked him and been impressed by him. How cool he was long before it was cool to be cool.

He smiled again. 'Good days, weren't they? I was never much good at sport but you were.'

I asked him who he remembered most and he rattled off Roy O'Neill, Peter Tate and Kathleen Clarke.

'Katie Clarke!' I almost shouted. 'I was totally in love with her. She used to get chapped lips but always seemed so grown up. She lived up the road from me in Battersby Road and I remember standing outside her gate one afternoon after school, not knowing what to do or say.

'There was a terrible silence until I asked her in desperation when her birthday was. November, she said. November? I said, I'm November! What date? Nineteenth, she said. Nineteenth, I roared. That's mine too! It was like we were married!'

'What happened after that?' asked Christopher.

'Well, nothing really,' I said. 'I was hopeless. Years later I got it into my head that the way forward with women was to make them laugh or at least talk to them, and that helped. But you're stuck with some things, I suppose. What about you? What are you up to?'

Christopher – he was never a Chris – flashed the same self-deprecating smile and said he was teaching creative writing at Durham University. It was some sort of holiday and he was visiting his parents in Honor Oak. His girlfriend, Helen, who also worked at the university, had headed north to Edinburgh for the break.

At that time, I told him, I was working for a semi-professional football club, coaching the junior lads and doing most of the writing for the match day programme. 'I really enjoy the writing,' I told Christopher. 'I write match reports and pen pictures of the players, and I try to make them more interesting than the usual guff, adding a touch of humour here and there and giving one or two players nicknames to brighten it all up – like The Grinch and Gargamel from The Smurfs, my assistant coach and a volunteer.'

Christopher seemed to take a real interest, which encouraged me to dive in further. I'm like that, given half the chance. 'To tell the truth,' I said, 'I'd love to write short stories. Not novels – they'd be beyond me. Just short ones with maybe a simple message and twist in the tail. D'you think I should join a creative writing class?'

'You could do,' said Christopher. 'You'd pick up some good tips, I'm sure. But you've already got the energy and enthusiasm from your match reports, so why not bash something out, about a thousand words? It's not a lot, once you get going. We can exchange emails and you can send them to me to have a look, if you like.'

I couldn't have been more pleased. Meeting Christopher Hadley and staying in touch. As we exchanged email addresses, Christopher added a little bit of advice: 'Why not think of people or situations that had a great or interesting effect on you or your life, whenever it was, and turn them into fiction?'

We shook hands firmly, and I said: 'Good idea, Christopher!'

About a thousand words. Not bad. Hope he likes it.

The sky blue suit

IN more ways than one he was the unlikeliest of mates, but I'm glad he was, grateful too.

Geoffrey Goodwin and I met for the first time at secondary school. He was already local to New Cross but I had to catch two buses from faraway Catford and knew absolutely no-one on that first morning, aged 11.

I sobbed that night but kept going to the 124 bus stop every morning. I'd never worn a school uniform before, so that was an added weight of the world as well.

Geoff had 10 or 11 mates from the primary school he had gone to a quarter of a mile down the road from the secondary school. So the new experience didn't knock him sideways like it did me.

He was a skinny kid with glasses, a proper coat hanger, but surprisingly good at tennis. There was a club near where he lived and he'd been going there since he was seven or eight, coached and everything.

I've been trying to think how we actually became mates, then it came to me – the pop music of the day. It took until just before the first Christmas break, by which time I was finally settling in, not happy but surviving. I was a Beatles fan and he was obviously pleased to point out a band that he thought was much cooler to follow, the Spencer Davis Group with an amazing singer called Stevie Winwood.

I can still see the superior grin on skinny Geoff's face at the time, and I had to admit that their song Gimme Some Loving was very impressive, not rock and roll but classier somehow, more grown-up rhythm and blues. Geoff suffered from quite a bad stutter and probably needed these little showoffy things to make him feel a bit better about himself.

There were some real brains in our 'A stream', but we were both very average. We found Bunsen burners boring, history even more so, and were distressed to find that the French teacher had a stutter worse than Geoffrey's. I still feel sorry recalling the teacher's attempts to explain how 'de le' became 'du'. His de le's were interminable. He must be long dead by now and the de le's with him. Rest in p-peace, Mr S-s-Simmons You were basically a very nice m-m-man.

The one subject Geoff and I both liked was English, and I regret to this day messing about so much in the lessons. The teacher, Mr David Croft in his sky blue suit, got really annoyed with me on one occasion and said I'd never get the GCE – which it was in those days. I spouted 'Yes, I will, sir', and I did. But that's no excuse.

The irony – isn't there always one? – was that Geoff and I were both pretty good at the short stories Mr Croft was so keen on. He encouraged the class to start with 200 words, then go on to 500 and then as many we liked but less than 3,000. 'You don't have to go over the top, young Silverside,' he called out to me. 'We get plenty of that already.

'The key is to capture the reader's attention in the first paragraph. Most readers, like Percival at the back there, want to drift off into their own worlds, put the book down and have a nice snooze. Don't you, Percival?'

'Pardon? Sorry, sir, I missed that.'

Mr Croft went on to say we just needed a general idea for the story first. Maybe choose something that happened during the summer holidays and turn it into fiction. 'You don't even have to worry about the ending,' he said. 'If you are well into your story and enjoying it, a good ending will almost always follow suit.'

Somehow I managed not to call out 'A sky blue suit, Sir?' and I remember him saying that a short, sharp twist in the tail was invariably a good ending to a short story; they go together.

You might be thinking by now, as this is obviously one of our short stories, that the meat of it – long before the twist in the tail – is that something befalls one of us, almost certainly skinny Geoffrey with his glasses and stutter. Perhaps he got into a fight and came off much the worst; a coma even.

But no, what happened, happened to me.

I lost half a leg. A car accident. Someone else was killed. I wasn't driving. I don't drive. I was 27. I also lost – gradually – my fiancé. I couldn't blame her. We're still friends. She's got two kids now, one of each. I'm godfather to the boy. Eddie.

Geoff and I had kept in touch and still saw each other once or twice a year. We had both passed Eng. and Eng. Lit. Mr Croft, in his sky blue suit, didn't have to say anything; he just smiled that smile of his. On the stairs one day I said I was sorry for being such a shit and he said something about how character forming it was. How kind. I didn't deserve it.

Geoff had moved to Cornwall three years before

the accident, working on boats of all things, plus a bit of tennis, coaching for the kids . When he heard about the accident he came straight to London and stayed a couple of nights in the flat. He arrived in the middle of one of my bad moments and we drank a fair bit, I have to admit.

We also talked a lot as well and I emphasised how I had lots of good moments too, how there were people much worse off than me, etc. My prosphetic left leg got me about well enough. I was working for the local theatre, doing their press reports, interviewing writers and directors, mainly for the local papers. I'd also got very close to a girl called Sandra, who was only 22 but already assistant artistic director at the theatre.

Geoff was clearly pleased to hear all this and glad that the only pistol on the premises was not for suicide but for the forthcoming panto. He also had a good idea that led to a modest but deep involvement in English Lit.

'What you've got to do, young Silverside,' he said, putting on the Mr Croft voice, 'is write a short positive story about a life-changing experience, around a thousand words or just over – or maybe even a play – and dedicate it to Mr David Croft.

'The title is obvious.'

The tears of Penelope Coomber

GERRY had a remarkable memory, mainly for faces but also for some names. Perhaps these things are triggered through life by different events, in this case Gerry's very first day at school.

He'd thought of it on innumerable occasions since, and now, nudging 40, it was there in his head again. It came to him and stayed there, clear as day. But it wasn't mainly about him. It was mainly about Penelope Coomber and the fact that she cried all day long on that first day.

Gerry could see her face and the tears like it was yesterday. Penelope was a very pretty name but Penelope, by unkind observations, wasn't a very pretty girl. She was already overweight and the curls around her very round face made it worse somehow.

We are born with instincts and insights. Some spiritual people think we actually choose our lives so that we can deal with the problems in our souls from previous incarnations. In other words no one was in that classroom by accident. It was all to do with Karma.

Gerry – 'Gerald' when he was four or five – knew that Penelope's pain had something to do with him, was linked to him, and no doubt with the others in the class as well. He remembered clearly how nervous he felt on that first day, going along to this place where his Mum would leave him for the first time. But Penelope's non-stop tears made it easier for him and for everyone else. (I'm not crying. We're not crying. Penelope's crying. We feel better than Penelope.)

There were two or three other things that Gerry could remember clearly from that day of days. The children were introduced in twos or threes to two long metal trays about eight inches deep. One contained water and the other sand. They were supposed to play with/in them. Gerald couldn't see the point and when it was his turn to play with them it was desultory to say the least.

Gerry remembered that first teacher – Mrs Herbert – very well, again as if she were standing next to him today. On that first day – and on many other days, he seemed to recall – she wore a big yellow dress like a huge smock that covered every inch of her, with tiny flowers splattered all over it. She was a big lady with a big black bun on the top of her head, but she didn't cry all day long. She was very gentle and kind and gave lots of attention to Penelope, which pleased us because the small classroom was quieter and there was therefore less attention paid to us.

The best part of the day for Gerald was at the end, not just 'going home time' but because Mrs Herbert almost always told a story. One he remembered from those early days was Rumpelstiltskin, which Gerald loved. How could anyone turn straw into gold? But Rumpelstiltskin could.

Mrs Herbert was a natural story-teller with her

soft, velvety voice. Little Gerald was transfixed and even Penelope Coomber must have been quiet during the telling because Gerald was transported to the very room where Rumpelstiltskin sat at his spinning wheel.

Home time brought on the wailing tears again as we were all picked up by our probably anxious Mums. We were all okay but Penelope wasn't. Again, comparisons helped the rest of us in our development.

As Gerry looked back yet again at that sandy, watered room through the prefontal cortex in the very front of his brain, another thought came to him.

Finding Penelope Coomber...

It was July, 2002, the school summer holidays. Gerry was an English teacher himself – thank you, Mrs Herbert! – and. with his wife Pam away on a month-long botanical holiday with Naturetrek in the Italian Dolomites, the timing was perfect.

Two other factors fitted in perfectly as well. The one friend from primary school he was still in contact with – ace batsman Roy O'Neill – had emailed suggesting the annual drink and curry. Even more congruous was the making of millions by Friends Reunited, the magical back bedroom website dreamed up not in Boston but in Barnet! The chances of tracking down Penelope Coomber were much healthier than they would be in 2020, Zuckerberg or no Zuckerberg.

Gerry told Roy O'Neill about Penelope Coomber and about trying to find her over two dhansaks – one prawn, the other chicken – and two large Cobras. Roy wondered why it had become such an obsession with Gerry as there was no playground romance involved. "It just had a big effect on me. I can see it now," said Gerry. "I can hear it now."

"Fair enough," said Roy, as easy-going as he always was at school. "Can I help?"

"Well," said Gerry. "If I do find out where Penelope Coomber is, I'd like to travel there and see her. I've got a month on my own and it would mean so much to me. And I wondered if you'd like to come. I know it sounds a bit mad but, if we're lucky, we might be able to tie it in with some local amusement."

"Wow," said Roy. "This goes deep. I don't even remember Penelope Coomber. I remember Catherine Hyatt and the two Clarkes, Janet and Kathleen...Katie."

"Nor do I apart from that first day," said Gerry. "I can only assume that things calmed down and she was more or less okay afterwards. I don't even remember what happened after Mrs Herbert's class. Perhaps we went to different classes and didn't see much of each other, apart from in the playground. This is all about that first day, which is absolutely rooted in me."

"I can see it is," said Roy. "Look into it, Gerry, and let me know if you find her and I'll be there. Let's just hope she lives somewhere near a racecourse!"

"Great idea," said Gerry, who loved the horses himself. "Wish me luck."

At home the following morning, he got down to look online. Years later, after all the dirty dealings across the world, such an exercise would be looked back upon as fun, positive and innocent. Certainly, Friends Reunited was a brilliant idea and doubtless brought thousands together.

Gerry quickly recognised names from 4A and 4B classes – Year 6 these days – and planned to contact three or four of them for fun, but no sign of Penelope Coomber. It didn't look good until he spotted Hilary Herbert, who was down as being former teacher Mrs Herbert's daughter.

By late afternoon they had emailed each other. Then they spoke by phone. Mrs Herbert had died 12 years earlier and Hilary said with pride that the school had placed a small plaque in her honour on the wall of what was now the reception class.

When Gerry asked tentatively about Penelope Coomber he expected a blank response but couldn't have been more surprised. "Mum actually took Penny under her wing from very early on," said Hilary, "and kept in touch throughout her time at the school. Penny did have confidence problems and Mum made sure her other teachers knew all about them, as well as seeing as much of her as she could."

"What about when she left primary school," asked Gerry. "Did you all lose touch?"

"We did," said Hilary. "It was inevitable, I suppose. Mum was getting older and had health problems herself, but she got a phone call out of the blue in the year that she retired.

"It was Penelope, aged about 20, saying she was getting married. She was pregnant but very positive about it all, saying that Paul was a good lad in a good job. They would start off living with his parents in Woodingdean, near Brighton."

Hilary had been given Penelope's address and gave it to Gerry, thinking he would write to her. Five days later, on the Saturday, Gerry and Roy O'Neill were parked opposite Penelope's – Penny's – home in Woodingdean.

They waited over an hour then watched as Penny pushed the pram towards the shopping centre with her daughter, aged about 11, walking beside her. So two children.

They followed them into Tesco's and saw them put fruit and biscuits into a basket like normal shoppers. The baby in the pram started crying but soon stopped as Penny picked it up with a big cuddle, swayed gently and covered it in kisses. The baby went back into the pram gurgling.

As Gerry put down his empty basket and went to leave the store, Roy O'Neill said to him: "I thought you wanted to meet her and talk to her."

"No, mate," said Gerry. "I just wanted to see something like that. I just needed to see something like that…"

Something's cooking for Danny

DANNY was like every other 14-year-old, and like every other 14-year-old he thought he felt it more acutely than anyone else.

His version was the need to make some kind of a leap in life. His mother did Tarot readings among four or five friends that met once at a fortnight for a delivery. Her favourite Zen card was 'Breakthrough', and that's what Danny knew he needed.

He was quite quiet without being shy but this kind of thinking led sometimes to what looked like daydreams. His English teacher, Mr Croft, was the one that called him out for not paying attention. "And what did the three witches promise Macbeth in the first instance then, Danny?"

'Thane of Glamis on top of Thane of Cawdor, Sir,' he answered, perhaps a little too hurriedly. He was tempted to add more about Macbeth's big mate, Banquo, but didn't want to be misunderstood as being cheeky to Mr Croft, who called everyone by their first name and was one of the few teachers he liked.

This was a typically minor incident that died without developing, and even that went into Danny's brain cells as something to work out. He didn't feel good or bad about it. He just felt a bit confused, yes, dreamy.

Life in Year 8 followed more or less the same pattern up to Christmas. Danny did enjoy drama and had one of the leading roles in the Christmas show. It made him feel good but it wasn't the magic he was after, and he knew it bothered him on one level or another.

He also liked writing, and it was Mr Croft who encouraged him to write more. In fact, it was with Danny in mind that the English teacher persuaded the head, Mr Bernham, to start the school's monthly magazine, Outspoken.

Mr Croft saw Danny as the editor or at least chief reporter. 'What I want,' he told the five-strong editorial team, 'is to get away from essays and school writing and produce a proper news magazine that highlights school initiatives but also gets out into the community and tells the stories out there. Hence, Outspoken.

'Let's interview the council leader and ask him what he's doing about the homeless people begging on the high street. Not how he feels but what he does about it! Let's go to the nearest foodbank and interview the staff and the people who need them. Get quotes, take pictures, campaign!'

Again, Danny got the point and did all that was asked of him with various skills and some new-found enthusiasm. He liked working on headlines and came up with a good one for the magazine's campaign to save the borough's bees from pesticides: Give Bees A Chance!

The first edition of the magazine was held up by the council leader at the next full council meeting as a good example of how young people in the borough were joining and even leading local initiatives. He wouldn't be so pleased with the next edition that exposed the growing army of beggars in the borough.

Danny interviewed one very articulate homeless woman on the situation – who went on to write a column for the magazine and suggested another headline that Mr Croft used: Beggar's belief!

The magazine was the talk of the staffroom. Mr Croft said how pleased he was with the editorial team and with Danny Wilkinson in particular. 'But the funny thing is,' she added, 'that Danny always seems deflated once the magazine has been produced. There's some kind of cloud over him.'

'Teenagers,' said Mr Simons, the social studies teacher, sipping his coffee. 'There's never been a cure.' One or two nods and sighs around the room quickly put an end to the conversation.

Danny carried on doing well at school. Most things came fairly easily to him and the extra stuff seemed to his parents to be exactly what he – and they – needed. His abilities included keeping any worries or anxieties to himself.

The only person Danny could really speak to was his younger sister, Phoebe, who was 12. They were mixed race – Dad black, Mum white – and they often chatted in the garden on bamboo chairs by the trampoline, drinking Coke Zero.

Danny put it as a question to her one Saturday morning. 'Feebs, d'you ever feel there's more to life than just this? I'm not unhappy or anything, I'm not even bored, I just feel kind of stuck between happy and sad. It is like a kind of boredom, but it's not boredom.'

'Not really, Dan' said Phoebe, 'but sometimes I feel I'm heading that way. Sometimes it's just a moment, or a feeling in a moment. It passes but it makes a mark.

When it happens, if it's like yours, I make sure I laugh about something, or make some kind of noise, or start messing about. It drives Mum mad.'

Danny was lucky to have Phoebe as a sister. They had always been close, without a trace of sibling rivalry. He supposed it was down to the slight age difference. Phoebe herself was just pleased her brother was a nice boy. She went to a different school and told her mates in Year 7. One or two had met Danny once or twice and smiled knowingly in that way of theirs.

'You'll feel better in the spring when the cricket starts,' she said to her brother, thinking of something, anything to say. Danny was okay at sport, which always helps, but more of a cricketer than a footballer. But he didn't think cricket would be the answer. He'd thought of that. In fact, the more he enjoyed something like cricket, the further away he seemed to be from what he called the leap, the breakthrough. This is getting weird, he said to himself.

'I need some kind of magic, Feebs,' he told his sister. 'I find it in books sometimes and in some music. Perhaps I need to write poems or learn the guitar or something. I'll ask Mr Croft what he thinks. He had a book published once, you know, a detective story. It couldn't have been that successful because he's still a teacher, but at least he did it. I admire him for that. He made the leap.'

Feebs put her Coke Zero on the bamboo table and said she was going on to the trampoline. As she got up, she said: 'You'll find it, brother, because you're looking for it. We had a Learning for Life lesson last week and that's what the teacher said, to find something the first thing you've got to be is looking.'

'That helps,' said Danny, sarcastically. 'I've been looking for 14 years and haven't really found anything yet. There's a line from an obscure song that keeps coming back to me: I've got a head full of questions, but I don't know who to ask.'

Over the next two or three weeks, Danny more or less forgot about his big search and was happier for it. He threw himself into the Christmas show, they were rehearsing twice a day, and really enjoyed it. He wasn't the star of the show or anything but loved the way everybody worked together to make it a success. There was a real buzz about it.

The school brought in Mr Mugnaioni, an actor/director from the local theatre, to put them through their paces and it made a big difference having a professional involved. They were treated like adults and felt like adults.

The theatre had a thriving youth section and Mr Mugnaioni said any of them would be very welcome to join. They had two shows a year in their studio theatre, in spring and autumn. 'Come along to taster sessions in February if you want to,' he told the class.

Danny and four others, three boys and a girl, said they would go along and give it a go. Mr Mugnaioni said he was more than pleased and would look forward to it after the school show, which was going very well.

Danny continued in the same comfortable vein through Christmas and into the new year, but the old rumblings started to re-emerge in the middle of January, a few days before his 15th birthday, which he would always remember.

He did join the youth group at the theatre, and he did enjoy it. One of the boys dropped out but Gary, Dharmesh and Lesley – the girl – were still keen and all four were chosen for the spring play, an adaptation of Dorian Gray.

Danny's parents and Phoebe went along and any

fears of a flop soon disappeared as the cast, obviously inspired and well trained by Mr Mugnaioni, received not a standing ovation but certainly a loud and enthusiastic one.

Danny and Feebs had one of their garden chats the next morning, a Saturday, the day before the team's first cricket practice – 'nets' as they called it. He was in the youth A team, batted a bit but was mainly a bowler – leg breaks and the occasional risky googly, which he tended to 'drag down' as the TV commentators call it.

'That was great last night, Dan,' said Feebs, who had just turned 12 herself and was growing up quickly. 'I was really proud of you and so were Mum and Dad. And cricket tomorrow...'

She didn't add anything else. She didn't need to. She knew – and Danny knew she knew – that the old demons were back. Well, not demons but definitely semi-demons. You couldn't say he was feeling sorry for himself, but he couldn't hide it either, and the last thing Feebs wanted to do was make a meal of what she saw as Danny's blues.

He took over the conversation. 'Maybe it's a family trait,' he said. 'Mum's brother Ron – uncle Ron – is a bit odd, don't you think? I've never been able to work him out, have you? Remember that crazy speech he made on Christmas morning? Maybe it's all mental.'

Feebs almost shouted her reply: 'No, it's not, Danny. If anything, you're too normal. And so am I. And so is uncle Ron. It's life, Danny, just bloody life!'

That was the nearest they ever came to a falling out. Feebs obviously had her own growing up to do and wisely decided not to repeat philosophical points about Danny having to look for something to find it. Let's keep it simple and straight-forward, she said to herself.

In March, as the first crocuses nodded good

morning, Danny made an odd but very good decision. He and Feebs had always liked cooking, so he joined the new after-school cooking and healthy eating class twice a week, not looking for anything except how to cook the perfect jerk chicken!

There were seven in the class, five girls and two boys. Danny was thankful for that. He wouldn't have minded being the only boy – he didn't suffer from any of that nonsense – but nevertheless he was glad that Kieran came along every Tuesday as well.

If anything – and surprisingly – Danny enjoyed it more than the theatre and the cricket. He found a wonderful simplicity in making tasty meals, especially spicy ones. He also found himself becoming more extrovert as the weeks went by, even making the others grin at silly remarks like Argee Bahjees.

One of the girls, Jenny, insisted that Danny's jerk chicken had to go in the slow cooker at lunchtime so that it would be perfect by about 4.30pm. She was right of course and everyone took some home, which pleased him no end.

Helping Danny seemed to come completely naturally to Jenny. What also came naturally to her one Tuesday, as they were last to leave the kitchen, was to reach up and kiss him quickly on the lips.

Breakthrough.

The twigs of democracy

SEEING that their big interest was entomology, maybe it wasn't such a surprise that their internal democracy was in danger of becoming a can of worms.

There were five sitting members of their standing committee that month, the odd number they all agreed making it easy for all concerned if it ever came to a vote.

And, for the first time, it did.

The apple cart, as well as the can or worms, was upset when Clare the Chair wanted to bring a sixth person on to the committee, a good mate of hers whose skills on the subject would make all the difference; take things forward; knew the job inside out; blah-di-blah.

The would-be sixth member, her colleague from work, was Carole with an 'e'. She was already a member of the group but Clare with an 'e' reckoned Carole with 'e' would help take the group in a new and exciting direction, 'freshen things up, help them see the trees for the wood.'

No one laughed. They'd heard that one so many

times in their little rustic association. Sam, as usual, was first to make her point. 'Trouble is,' she said. 'Clare will definitely add something to the committee, but there'll be six of us and I think five works better. Democratically.

'That's what they do on the Supreme Court in America.'

'They have nine,' said Leroy, who knew everything.

'Same argument, an odd number,' said Sam before anyone else started barking.

Clare said she didn't know what Samantha meant. 'Well, it's pretty obvious,' said Sam. 'Most of our decisions don't amount to a hill of dead wood and leaves, but we might have an issue that crops up that causes some level of consternation.'

'Consternation?'

'Consternation,' Sam repeated, 'and on occasions like that we need to have an odd number on the committee, five not six. Or seven, not eight. So that the vote matters. Our annual trip to the New Forest, for example'

Clare pulled one of her faces. 'I can't for the life of me see the difference between five, six or seven, or 10 or 11, come to that, when we've all got what's best for the group in mind.'

'That's not the point,' said Leroy. He was the real expert on the subject, the one they all generally referred to, and they couldn't afford to lose him, organisationally or technically, if things got out of hand. 'With a committee of five we know that the voting works if it comes to a vote. Unanimous. Four to one. Or three to two. And everyone goes home happy, looking forward to our weekends among the insects.'

'We already go home happy,' declared Clare.

'Yes. Because there's five of us,' said Dhooper, who invariably spoke last and least. 'We haven't had any big issues, not even Ron's resignation really – he was always looking for the exit – but we've still used three votes to two on a couple of occasions, and no one blew their tops afterwards.'

'Because Clare was always one of the three,' said Rose, Ron's wife. 'When has she ever been one of the two? And I resent Dhooper's remark about my husband. He served this committee for seven years and is still a valued and active member where it matters, out there among the shrubs.'

'Sorry, Rose,' said Dhooper. 'You're quite right and I'd like my apology to be included in the minutes.'

'No one does the minutes properly since Ron resigned,' said Rose. 'And we're drifting from the point. What I'd like to know is what happens if we have a sixth member and there's ever a three-three vote.'

'Normally, the chair then has the casting vote,' said Dhooper. It was not hard to see him moving up from deputy chair to chair at the next AGM in April. He was a born leader and, they could all sense, quite ambitious in the group approaching its tenth year.

'So intrinsically it would be the same as a three-two vote that we've got at the moment,' said Rose with some feeling, 'with Clare still very much in charge.'

'That's how things work,' said Leroy.

'They do,' said Dhooper.

'As always,' Leroy added, stifling a grin.

They had all kept their comments to a minimum, short and sharp, I suspect, because we were all wondering where Rose got 'intrinsically' from. Then Carole with an 'e' walked in.

'Hi, all,' she beamed. 'Sam invited me along. Hope you don't mind.'

'Well, you should really be coming up under A.O.B.,' said Dhooper, showing once again his chair-like qualities. 'But as long as everyone is happy…'

'Shall we have a vote on it?' asked Leroy, stifling another grin.

'No, I really don't think that's necessary,' said Clare with a clip. 'We won't be deciding anything tonight anyway. I just wanted you to meet Carole and hear about her considerable qualities on the subject, her new ideas and about the various other committees she's served on.'

'So no vote, casting or otherwise?' slipped in Leroy, overdoing it a bit.

Carole with an 'e' moved her eyes from one person to another and said: 'Look, I think it's best if you have a discussion amongst yourselves and let me know later how you feel. It really doesn't matter much to me. I've got a very busy life already. But I can find time for this.'

With that she picked up her handbag and left brusquely, asking Clare on the way out if they were all still on for the study at Bostall Heath on Sunday morning.

'Definitely,' said Sam, answering for Clare. 'We should all be there. Let's have a drink afterwards. I think I'll need one.'

The meeting did in fact finish with a vote on whether Carole with an 'e' should join the committee, and it was carried by three votes to two, Clare, Sam and Dhooper in favour. Leroy voted with Rose so that hers wasn't the only hand up against.

'The important thing,' said Dhooper – once again displaying excellent leadership qualities – 'was that we all carry on in the field (his little joke) that means so much to the committee and our 27 members.'

Dhooper was right. Entomology was the thing, democracy or no democracy. No point getting ants in their pants.

The Orange Menace

LOOKING down from the top deck of the bus, I could tell that if he wasn't trouble itself he was certainly looking for it.

He was tall, skinny, balding and menacing in a tight-fitting yellow T-shirt with different colour blotches on it, carrying a can of some sort, probably strong lager. He wasn't exactly ginger. It looked more like he'd painted his hair orange, what there was left of it in his mid-to-late-thirties.

I couldn't work out why the bus was taking so long to drive away from the stop. Perhaps the driver had been told to wait there to adjust his schedule, the way they have to sometimes, but there was no announcement.

The grinning Orange Menace was making great play of allowing people on to the bus before him, even bowing ostentatiously in front of them, but I got the feeling he'd attack anyone who made a comment or even looked him in the eye.

You know the type. Silent but violent.

Three or four people walked past him on to the bus, avoiding his eyes, but still it didn't move. Suddenly, the winter sun seemed to make his head glow like the Martian I remembered from a film in my childhood. I was only seven and had nightmares for months afterwards.

The next moment the Orange Menace was obviously listening to something the driver was saying, protected by Perspex. Like, possibly, get on the bus, please sir, I'm just about to move off.

A threatening grin from the Orange Menace said that the driver might expect being perfectly safe behind the Perspex, but he shouldn't really think he was. It was a well-practised, threatening smile that had obviously worked before in different places and scenarios.

You've guessed it, the Orange Menace finally came upstairs. I was sitting three-quarters of the way back on the left-hand side, which is why I was able to spot the him and the hoo-ha at the stop in the first place.

At the front upstairs was a pleasant old lady with two young lads, probably her grandsons out for the day, which was suddenly getting dark. Maybe they'd been to the park. I could tell she was pleasant because her body language towards the two boys was wonderfully inspiring. I'm easily moved by such things.

Four or five seats up from me, over on the right side, was a black man minding his own business. Looking at his back and his face as he looked out the window for something or someone, I quickly registered that he could be turned to in a crisis. He looked cool and muscular, like a West Indian fast bowler.

The Orange Menace, predictably, made a meal of walking towards the back of the bus, past me, and back again before noisily sitting down and spreading himself out aggressively two seats in front of me, the mad grin still on his face.

Three secondary schoolboys, of Asian backgrounds, had come upstairs at the previous stop. Two of them sat across the aisle from me, two seats up, and the third two seats further on to give himself a bit more space to read, possibly for an exam.

I didn't turn to check these facts, as you can well imagine. I didn't want the Orange Menace thinking I was checking him or anything out. I thought the best tactic was to keep my head looking forward, seemingly unthinking.

I often carry a book to read on public transport – the latest the recommended 'A Prayer for Owen Meany' – but not on this short journey, five more stops, four if we zoom past the request stop over the road from the dentist and the Chinese take-away.

The Orange Menace started talking, not in tongues but certainly oddly. I couldn't hear the words clearly. Perhaps he was talking on his mobile. Perhaps he'd already had a few. Perhaps he knew that it would irritate people. Then he started this weird, tuneless whistle, obviously part of his regular performance.

A few quiet seconds then went by before the Orange Menace went walkabout again. First he walked forward so that he was two seats in front of the muscular black man and one in front of the secondary schoolboy who was sitting on his own across the aisle. I must say that neither he nor his mates were taking much notice of the Orange Menace, which was a good thing.

Nor was the muscular black man, who sat there perfectly calmly as the Orange Menace got up again, chuckling now, and went to sit near the two Asian schoolmates. Again, we all just ignored him. The best policy. But then it went up a gear.

The Orange Menace got up again and sat in the seat across the aisle from me, with his feet out, facing me but managing to lean forward. 'Got a light, mate?' he said with that same grin.

'A light what?' I asked him steadily. He was not amused but pleased that he'd provoked someone at last and would see some action and possibly some blood. He asked me again and I replied with an unembellished 'No'. I didn't need to add that smoking was not allowed on the bus.

I should tell you at this point something about myself. Over the last 15 or 20 years, whenever I have some kind of nightmare, I deal with the threat, be it a grizzly bear, a rabid dog or a gangster with a gun, by simply clobbering the opposition.

So when the Orange Menace lunged at me, I knocked him clean out.

The 'lino' and the star player

IN those days the referee's assistant was what he really was, the lineman – the 'lino' – and the star player was the star player, none of this 'No. 10' nonsense.

So this is about the star player who disagreed with the 'lino' and called him a four-letter word that wasn't love. The lino put down his flag gently on the turf, went a few yards on to the pitch and knocked the star player out.

This lino – still slightly plumper than he should have been – had been working out every day to improve his fitness and must have got carried away, as was the star player.

The lino was almost middle-aged and had never really made it as a referee at the top level. He'd never been as fit and strong and was obviously troubled somewhere upstairs. Unmarried. Unsuccessful.

Linos take a lot of stick, more than referees actually because they are closer targets, especially at grounds built a hundred years ago that had touchlines just a few yards from the crowd.

This lino, whose name was Potts, remembered a yoghurt that hit the back of the neck at The Den and oozed down his black shirt. He ignored it to concentrate on the play and not be put off, earning the referee's patronising pat on the back after the game.

This latest incident caused a sensation, making the front pages as well as the backs and being discussed ad nauseum on television and radio. Potts was interviewed by all sundry but the star player – embarrassed, I suppose – always refused to say a word on the subject. He just wanted it to go away.

The match referee became famous as the first official in the history of the game to send off his lino. The two protagonists left the field together, one causing the crowd to erupt in jeers and cheers, the other slowly coming round on a stretcher.

Potts faced an FA inquiry and was banned from league football for life. He was still allowed to officiate at Sunday morning football matches, where he earned a reputation as one of the best refs around, no doubt because of his experience at the higher level.

It took a long while for the star player to be seen as a star player again. The incident badly shook his confidence, which wasn't helped by away crowds counting him out every time he was in possession of the ball. He grew a beard and exposed his tattoos for the media, but it's true to say he was never the same star player again.

What made it worse for the star player was one of the tabloids taking Potts' side after the incident and turning him into some kind of anti-hero, the ordinary joe who was sick and tired of 'referees' assistants' being seen more as shop assistants by millionaire footballers.

Potts did well out of it as well, signing a lucrative contract with a tabloid to give his opinions every week on 'Footballers' Fatal Foibles' in the Premier Division.

A jealous tabloid rival tried to denigrate the lino under the headline Potts Of Money, but if anything it served to make him even more popular. Good luck to him, was the consensus.

Happily, the star player gradually found his feet again and, clean shaven, he helped his team to the top four and a place in Europe. He also adopted a self-deprecating approach to life which everyone appreciated. His recovery from the incident was almost total.

By the time he hung up his boots, the star player had become a natural for television and the incident actually worked in his favour because of his ability to laugh at himself. He accepted a weekly shift on Sky Sports and was sometimes referred to sarcastically as Rocky by the rest of the panel.

The lino's life quietened down as well as each year passed – his latent gift being to train young referees to always keep their cool – but the controversial incident was inevitably recalled on the day that Mr Potts died alone from a sudden stroke.

The star player was asked to reflect on the incident 15 years earlier. 'We never actually met after what happened,' said the star player. 'I still don't understand why he got so angry about being called a fool. It was definitely a corner and not a throw-in.'

Postcode problems

I TOOK the daily tablet, Lanzaprazole, 30-meg, with half a small glass of water but knew I'd still need a pee inside five minutes.

The thought is irritating because I'd then be on my way downstairs to pierce and microwave the cherry tomatoes to go with the peanut butter on toast for the two of us, crunchy me, smooth her.

And I'd developed the perfect routine: microwaving the toms first because they'd eventually cool down; putting the kettle on; getting the butter and semi-skimmed milk from the fridge; putting her slices and then mine – sourdough to please the Lanzaprazole – into the Russell Hobbs toaster; two plates and two cups from the top cupboard; two knives and two forks from the drawer.

Maybe an extra slice of toast each for Oxford marmalade. My old history teacher, a bit of a snob but very likeable with his confident grin and crinkled Fifties hairstyle, swore by it.

There was a kind of joy involved in this routine every morning – there's some kind of joy in everything that works well, imo – but, at the same time, it's awful to know that the need for a wee – that single-minded tingle from below – would interrupt the routine as always.

The thing to do is pour the boiling water into the tea cups as the pierced toms are being obliterated for two minutes, and zip back upstairs, knowing that the tea (hers decaffe), would benefit from standing a few seconds while I'm otherwise engaged.

There's a tiny toilet downstairs, next to the kitchen, under the stairs, but it's not been working properly for months and there's a no entry sign on it for visitors. Mend it? I'm no handyman.

On that particular day I wasn't going into the office. I was one of three reporters covering three areas – Lewisham, Greenwich and Bexley – for the local paper. I took the morning off for the latest whim of a job interview. It was a Thursday, the day the paper came out, so there was no panic. I liked the job, loved it actually, but I was always on the lookout for something else, something different. That's me to a tee, I suppose, whimsical.

I drive my wife mad by starting explanations arse-upwards. So when you ask me what the new job is, instead of just telling you I drive you mad as well by saying that, well, I've always been fascinated by postmen. Once, when much younger, I would have fancied a spell as one of the kings of the road, the heroes of the highway. So – to finally get to the bloody point – was I finally applying to be a postman?

No.

What it was – she hates that introduction to a sentence as well – I'd seen a job advertised in the journalists' magazine called Journalist. Sports editor required for the Post Office magazine called Post Haste. Actually, that was my little joke. I like playing with headlines.

It was about 1995 and I can't remember what the magazine was called. Today, if you can believe it, it's called One Magazine. Picture the committee that decided that. In Greenwich they changed the name of a popular community-wide sports association to 'Better'. Nothing else, just Better. Bloody Better! It's not better, it's worse!

Anyway, to get back to somewhere near the point, if you're walking along with two Post Office magazines and someone happens to ask you what they are, you might say: 'Two One Magazines'.

My wife also hates that as well, me going off at tangents – digressions like Holden Caulfield's – but I find it entertaining. To be fair, she mimics me brilliantly at it. Word for word and exactly the same rhythm and emphases. Has me in stitches, she does. In fact, once...

Anyway, that morning I went for the job interview, having covered a fair bit of sport at the local paper and played a bit myself. Left foot a wand. If they had their own football or cricket team I'd be straight in there, first wicket down and box to box from midfield. I was in my early 30s, in my prime. Captain material.

Actually, there was a time, when was it exactly...?

Sorry. The interview was at 11am at, of all places, the Post Office Tower, now the BT Tower, at 60 Cleveland Street. Had never been up there, so it'd be an experience if nothing else. Completed in 1964, the tower is 177 metres high (581ft), excluding the further section of aerial rigging that brings the total height to 189 metres (620 feet).

I left really early. I always leave really early. You never know what might hold you up; work on the line; a suicide on the track; a fight in the ticket office; a tube strike. Eighteen months earlier, I did some freelance work for a Finnish magazine – sport again – where I had to travel to the Midlands for First Division football games. I used to get to the Midlands by noon for 3pm kick-offs, knowing I could have a light lunch and read a le Carre over coffee.

One Saturday, I kid you not, the speeding train suddenly lurched to a screeching halt in a wide open expanse of field, somewhere near Snitterfield, I think it was. Then, as we all watched, two members of the train staff were seen chasing a man, obviously a miscreant, across the field. The train was 45 minutes late but I was still in good time for the Sky Blues v Villa. So, take the point, young journos, always leave really early.

Back to the tower. Are you nervous for me, even so long after the event? D'you think it went horribly wrong? Well, actually, it did and it didn't.

I asked at the desk at the bottom of the tower and was told I had to go to the 34th floor, or very near the top anyway. Might have been the 28th. I got there and was asked to wait, alone, in this very small waiting room. I was early, 10.50 – I'm always really early, as explained – and sat there until summoned at 11.10.

Now, I don't know if you've got a good idea about the kind of personality, or temperament, you're dealing with here, but at times like that I tend to get a bit light-headed and very much see the funny side of things. So there I was, on the 34th or 28th floor of the Post Office Tower, eventually shaking hands with this serious old, bald, boring, suited bloke acting like the Home Secretary's secretary.

We sat and chatted amiably enough and I told him how I'd always admired postmen and almost became one myself at one point. That wasn't true but it's good to colour stuff up at times like that. He didn't look over-impressed and the interview stalled somewhat.

I filled one awkward silence successfully by telling my story about the shy man who joined a stamp collecting society that took him all over the world. 'Philately will get you everywhere,' I announced, laughing at my own joke.

Then, suddenly – desperately? – he asked me a question that brought out the full force of my whimsy.

What did I think of the new postcodes?

'I'm glad you asked me that,' I said. 'I think it's yet another example of people's lives being invaded by numbers. Bank numbers, insurance numbers, tax numbers, phone numbers, bus numbers, back numbers, wrong numbers...what's wrong with SE12? Who needs 9HY added? What's 9HY anyway when it's at bloody home?'

Didn't get the job.

Ring them bells!

BIG Ginger was a constantly cheerful betting shop manager who looked as if he'd just ridden the last winner himself. Albeit carrying overweight.

Inevitably, he attracted all sorts of characters to the shop tucked away just off Deptford High Street, shaded by the most beautiful magnolia tree.

One such character – a proper regular – was old Albert, 'Albie' to his mates and family but always Albert, addressed in measured, respectful tones by Big Ginger.

At the time of this story, Albert was 73 if he was a day, and the short pensioners' 53 bus ride to the shop on Saturday morning was a highlight of his week. Necessarily a frugal chap, he laid out £2.60 on his particular bet, every penny of it in Big Ginger's shop.

His bet was an old-fashioned Super Yankee, none of this new-fangled Lucky 15 nonsense they were just bringing in and much-favoured by Victor, a lovely big black guy with a grin to match.

More than once Victor tried to point out the benefits of the Lucky 15 to old Albert, as opposed to those of the Super Yankee. They both tended to pick out long shots at big prices and Victor argued in favour of the enhanced odds available on just one Lucky 15 winner. But no thanks, Albert stuck to his Super Yankee.

To the uninitiated – and there must be many of you – old Albert's Super Yankee covered FIVE selections, making 26 x 10p bets – 10 doubles, 10 trebles, five four-horse accumulators and one five-horse accumulator. £2.60, okay? Do the maths or Google it if you need to make it clearer.

Anyway, the most old Albert ever won was about fifty quid for getting three winners, three doubles and a treble if you can work that out, a pretty good pay-out because his horses were always 10 to 1 or more.

But on this particular Saturday in late October…

'Another Super Yankee?' beamed Big Ginger as he took old Albert's betting slip with handwriting that was beyond the abilities of his younger – and, to be honest, less interested – assistants. Big Ginger always gave old Albert three quid change from a fiver, both knowing the simple gesture would remain their little secret, the bookie making up the 60p difference himself.

'Why don't you at least try a Lucky 15 with your outsiders,' said Victor, plucking his slip from the holder. 'The bumped up prices of the winners is the key, my man!'

Old Albert smiled but took no notice for the 100th time and proceeded to pick out his five selections from the three meetings – Ripon (high draw best in sprints) and Kempton Park on the flat, and Chepstow over jumps. It had been hissing down for a couple of days all over the country but all three meetings passed 'precautionary inspections'.

Victor's day started with two greyhound defeats at

Crayford, the tight track in Kent, but his main bet – the Lucky 15 – was yet to come. And how it went!

His first runner won at 8 to 1, the second at 12 to 1 and the third at 13 to 2. He was already assured of one of his best-ever returns, but if the fourth horse won in the 4 o'clock at Chepstow he was looking at thousands for his £15 total stake.

'Massive!' beamed Big Ginger. 'I think it must be the rain that's stopping all the favourites. And I'll tell you what, old Albert's 10p's are not doing so bad either. His first three have come in as well!'

They talked as if old Albert wasn't there – which he wasn't.

He preferred to catch the 53 home to watch the races on telly, especially as it was starting to get nippy. His sons, Alex and Terry, had bought him Sky Sports for the football and cricket – he loved his sport – and of course the horse racing.

He'd make himself a couple of bacon rolls to go with the strong tea, no sugar, and settle into his old armchair by the gas fire…heaven.

Needless to say, he was buzzing when his first three horses stormed home, slapping his armrests with both hands as they passed the post and knowing he'd already won 50 times his layout stake of £2.60 (two quid thanks to Big Ginger).

And when his fourth horse hit the front on the bridle in the 3.45 at Ripon, he knew that Big Ginger and Victor would also be going bananas on his behalf in the betting shop. Big Ginger always related old Albert's results to his customers, most often in subdued or groaning tones.

But not this time!

Old Albert had become quite good at maths, thanks in large to horse racing, and he quickly worked out that he had no less than £210 going on to his fifth and last selection, Sandy Special, at the early price of 12 to 1, in – you've guessed it – the 4 o'clock at Chepstow.

Which meant that Victor and old Albert couldn't both win the lot.

Or could they?

The 4 o'clock at Chepstow was a three-mile handicap chase and, as everyone knows, Chepstow's going gets very heavy after persisting rain. 'Hock-deep' is one expression, 'bottomless' another.

Luckily, Victor's horse – Ring Them Bells – was a renowned stayer and couldn't have it soft enough, 'stayed longer than the mother-in-law' as one pundit used to put it, and was backed from 15 to 2 to clear 4 to 1 favourite.

Pretty soon Victor was shouting and hollering, along with Big Ginger and the whole of the betting shop.

In his own over excitement, old Albert had gone upstairs to the bathroom and then put the kettle on for a second cuppa he didn't get to drink, and by the time he returned to his armchair they were already racing in the 4 o'clock at Chepstow.

It was a long race and pretty soon three-quarters of the field were covered in mud. All old Albert could do to recognise his selection was to turn up the commentary to find out where Sandy Special was in the field behind the cantering Ring Them Bells.

The seven-year-old mare didn't get a mention, not even as a faller or a horse that had been 'pulled up'.

Oh, well, thought old Albert, I'll just have to make do with £210, a familiar regular punter's lament after being close to a really big win. He'd pick it up on Monday, treat himself to lunch and slip Big Ginger a tenner for a drink and for always being so kind.

Big Ginger it was who rang old Albert's bell an

hour later, the first time he'd ever done it. Beaming as usual, he said: 'Here's your winnings then, Albert, roughly one thousand 150 quid. Didn't want you to wait till Monday for it.'

Old Albert took the cash in a daze. 'I expected £210,' he stammered. 'That would have been...'

Big Ginger interrupted: 'No, mate. Sandy Special was a late withdrawal because of the heavy going so your bet went on the returned favourite, as per the rules.'

'Ring Them Bells?' said a still dazed old Albert.

'Ring Them Bells!' said Big Ginger.

Leaving Tom to Tom

THE only thing I can tell you for sure about Tom is his first name, Tom.

He's a real person but, because he keeps most of himself to himself – including his last name – I'll have to add a bit of fiction here and there to try to get across how great he is.

Greatness? How on earth are we supposed to judge? We can fall back on all sorts of words and phrases – kindness, generosity, friendship, a person to trust and/or treasure – but how do you really hit home?

Well, it's not that hard actually. Almost every approach works as long as you mean it. People get it. People understand. People feel a bit better for hearing about people like Tom, especially about Tom.

All of us have special people in our lives, but how many merit an essay? Tom is in that category. I actually feel better myself as the words about him tumble after each other.

Tom cuts our grass, plants the odd handful of

seeds. You wouldn't really call him a gardener. Mainly he tidies gardens. Ours is one of about 12 gardens he tidies once a month or so, which means he does three or four a week, I suppose, on top of the various odd jobs he does for his church. They call on him as we do, by text, and know, as we do, that he'll always turn up on his trusty old bike.

Give or take a hail Mary, Tom's a Catholic, but there's nothing the least bit nutty about him. Meet him for the first time, there's no way you could assume anything about him. Not a thing.

The thing you'll get to notice soon enough, though, is the glow. Tom glows. If you tried to pin him down about it, the way I like to do with interesting people, you wouldn't get anywhere. We've tried in our devious ways to get to the bottom of it, but it's impossible. He just glows and that's it, like Jesus does.

The surname? He keeps it to himself, I reckon, because he doesn't want you to use it in any way at all. Not a Christmas card; certainly not a birthday card (he let slip he'll be 61 in September). He'll tell you the area where he lives but not the address.

He hasn't got a telly. He loves to read. And you know those ladies you meet at elderly social gatherings, some club or other, old people's homes or sheltered accommodation; that kind of thing? One thing you notice is that the ladies, in particular, are on the look-out for a partner or a special acquaintance (have you been there?), as if they finally know the score in their sixties and what they're looking for. Well, if Tom ever showed his ever-smiling but not facetious face at such a place, with his full head of slightly ginger hair, he'd absolutely knock them out, one after another. They'd stand no chance against the glow (not that he'd ever deem to put himself in that situation).

Do you need more about the glow? Well, as I think about it, all I can say that it is totally, totally natural. Tom's glow I can picture among the crowd making its way to the Mount for the Sermon. It would show the way, across the road like the ultimate Lollipop Man.

You know the way you want certain people to be happy, or even happier by meeting someone, some kind of partner (as in two paragraphs ago)? Well, we used to feel that, sense that, more or less, about Tom. What we should have done and slowly learned to do, which I suppose we have, was to leave Tom totally to Tom. We realised there was a kind of perfection about him, attached to him, that needed nothing from us apart from the three cups of tea and Kit-Kat chats and laughter that broke up his expert and tireless tidying among the weeds.

However – and if ever a story could do without a 'But' or 'However', it's this one – last week I followed Tom at a respectful distance on the mountain bike our grandson left over the weekend. I shouldn't have done it. I feel ashamed. I felt bad on the bike for wanting to know exactly where Tom lived. I should have known better. I should have learned from Tom. Instead I kept peddling (if that's how you spell it).

He turned off the high street and right again at a small side road. I was about 50 yards behind him, but as I turned right there was no sign of him ahead.

All I could see was some kind of glow...

God's great sense of humour

THE funny thing about Freddie Mackie's faith was how he frequently liked to explain what he called God's great sense of humour, at least as it struck Freddie Mackie.

Freddie, in his 40s now, had always been one of those indefatigable, full-of-life characters, and he saw it, in his own uncomplicated way, as a gift from above. His faith was also of the simple kind, full of easy acceptance and spiritual good humour and confidence.

Freddie liked to help people in all sorts of different ways – gardening, running errands, listening, making them laugh or think, very occasionally a shoulder to cry on – but he never made a meal of it or them. That would completely spoil it for others and for him, take away the point of the whole exercise, be almost self-defeating.

He went to church once or twice a week but again without overdoing any of it. The one strong opinion he had was that – given the chance – he would turn at least part of his church into a regular home for the local homeless. Even then he kept his opinion more or less to himself. He didn't see the point in climbing to the top of the steeple with a megaphone.

But what he did like, as I say, was to share with people his love of what he called God's great sense of humour. 'What it is,' he'd say, 'is that God obviously has a sense of humour simply because He's the best at everything else. Kindness, empathy, great ideas, great understanding. He sheds tears for us when it rains and the sense of humour comes out mostly in sunshine.

'And what's more,' exclaimed Freddie to his latest would-be converts on the subject, raising his voice in great passion and his face and eyes aglow, 'I can prove it!'

He was talking this time to an elderly West Indian couple, Chandresh – 'Lord of the Moon' – and Binita – 'Humble and unassuming' – two parishioners who tended to be a bit more literal in their beliefs but came to greatly enjoy Freddie's sudden outbursts on the subject.

Freddie's 'proof' went like this: 'What happens is, I get the feeling – a message to the soul through the heart and brain – walking along the pavement, say, to the shops, the local Co-op. Or sometimes even before I go out, and the feeling tells me that I'm going to meet someone interesting who amuses or interests me in one way or another. A good example is a philosophic man who loves to talk and talk, and loudly. People call him Dave but he tells me his real name is Dennis.

'I hadn't seen him for ages, I was almost worried about him, but then suddenly, thanks to the feeling, there he was, sitting outside the Full English café, drinking a flat white. I bought one and joined him at the small, flowered table. "Freddie," he said straight away, "the world's gone wrong. It's gone mad. The politicians are taking us for a ride and they don't care…"

'He always carries on in that vein for about 10 minutes or so before he allows me a word in edgeways. I, of course, try to encourage him to find the positive things in life instead. Then, like clockwork, he likes to adopt exactly the same approach and tells me about visiting a friend in hospital or a long walk in the countryside. That's the spirit, Dennis, I say, and suddenly he's smiling and talking about the horses. We both like a flutter now and then.'

Binita then asked Freddie how exactly God's great sense of humour played a part in all that. 'Well, good question,' said Freddie. 'It's obvious to me. I get the feeling and then the feeling becomes something concrete, like Dennis swapping his demagoguery for a sea of smiles. Or sometimes God just makes me laugh. I'll get the feeling, walking along, and seconds later I'll see something funny, someone in a big funny hat with about six Co-op full-up carrier bags running for a bus...which the person always catches.

'I'll also tell you a very strange thing as well. It's got to the point where I walk along and actually ask God to provide something to surprise me or make me laugh. Like a bonus. And I'll tell you what, it happens every time. Sometimes I forget that I've asked Him, I get diverted by something or other, and am doubly surprised and delighted when it happens two minutes later, often a very welcome mobile phone call with good news out of the blue 'That was it,' I grin to myself and look up and wave to the clouds.

Freddie gave Binita and Chandresh two more examples. One he called 'a regular' and the second 'a real cracker'. The regular is about a rather miserable, slow-walking character who lives down the same road as Freddie. 'I ask Him one of my asks and this character appears from around the corner, walking home. I always call 'Good morning!' and he has to reply even though he probably doesn't want to. At least he makes one positive contribution to the day by being forced to say good morning. Or even just a nod!'

A 'recent cracker' was all about Good Friday and Freddie himself. Freddie's wife, Sandra, was out for the day with her best friend, Lesley, so the thought came into Joe's head about a flutter on the horses. He might even join Dennis in the local betting shop. But this time he got not one of his good feelings but a sudden bad or worrying feeling. He shouldn't be having a bet on Good Friday. He should reflect and then wait until Bank Holiday Monday when there are lots of horse race meetings to choose from.

He was still tempted to join Dennis in Paddy Power's and tried to justify it to himself – as we all do – by asking forgiveness beforehand, or saying going there was good for Dennis, or maybe even leaving the prayer until after the betting. We've all been there, trying to kid God as well as ourselves. It never works.

So what did Freddie do? The feeling came as usual and with it the solution! He looked at the runners online – televised Newcastle and Lingfield, two of his favourite tracks – and picked his usual five horses across the two cards. But…instead of having a bet he just watched them all on television with a cuppa and two toasted hot cross buns with plenty of butter.

He felt wonderful about this simple but incredible solution to a spiritual problem – picking out the horses but not betting on Good Friday – and grinned to himself about God's great sense of humour.

All five horses won, of course.

Young Mr Dexter and shy Miss Bright

LIKE many a romance, it didn't get off to the best of starts.

'You're 15 minutes early,' she said at the front desk after he gave his name. 'Golly,' he said, 'I thought you were going to say I was 15 minutes late. Phew. Don't worry, I've got a book.'

She shuffled some papers and said: 'Please sit and wait', indicating two rows of seven leather chairs about 10 yards behind him. He sat in the middle of the front row, stifling a chuckle.

Seven and a half minutes later she spoke so that he could hear her clearly: 'Mr Dexter, third floor.'

'But I'm Mr Dexter,' he grinned.

'I know you are,' she said, not finding him the least bit funny. 'Mr Stonebridge's office is along the corridor on the right hand side. His name on the door.'

'Thank you very much,' said young Mr Dexter, deciding to leave the jousting there. If anything, his horse normally got more fed up than he did.

The interview went really well. Mr Stonebridge, the book publishers' senior editor, seemed to take to him without needing to suggest young Mr Dexter was over-qualified for the job.

He was 23 at the time, Mr Dexter was, and had a double first in English Lit, more than enough to satisfy Mr Stonebridge's urgent need for a junior to join his six-strong editorial team, especially as he wouldn't be allowed to get near any mistakes for the first three months or so.

Typical of him in those days, young Mr Dexter had to mention to Mr Stonebridge as he left the room how friendly and efficient the young lady on the front desk had been. 'Oh, Miss Bright,' he said. 'Yes, she's a lovely girl if still a bit shy. We all took a while to get to know her, but she'll prove a boon, I'm sure.'

Young Mr Dexter wasn't at all shy but was annoyed by that fact that he'd been buggering about for the previous 18 months since leaving uni and needed to take stock of himself and his life. Join the game, as he put it.

He spent the next three months more or less proof reading until Mr Stonebridge, presumably pleased enough, asked him to start work on a particularly scruffy ghost-written biography from the sporting world.

One or two sets of eyes in the long, narrow office rolled at the promotion, but to Roger Dexter it meant some real work he was desperate to get into.

The auto-biography, typically, was credited to a retiring professional footballer well known for his midfield machismo as well as his limited vocabulary. His 'ghost' writer was a long-term hanger-on in the football/television world, so the unofficial working title 'Foul Is Fair" was used for general amusement around the office.

The hanger-on's chosen title – after it had all been

knocked into some sort of shape by young Mr Dexter, helped by one of the senior editors – was the euphemistic 'Taking One for the Team', and it went on to sell surprisingly well.

Two more years went by like a le Carre page turner, both of them surprisingly enjoyable for not-so-young Mr Dexter. Three of the five other hacks, who had taken to him by now, were ex-Fleet Street, so there was never a dull or totally sober moment. They all knew professionally that less was more, working to tighten everything up to make it more readable.

If one of them, Keith Fisher, had got hold of this particular story before it went to press, you could be sure it would be at least 50 words shorter and better...in other words, 50 words shorter.

Don't get the idea those two years were spent like four or five in The Sun newsroom without a saved soul in sight. Far from it. The company – Crossheads Limited – did some community stuff, including two matches a year – one football, one cricket – for Great Ormond Street.

And you'll be pleased and surprised to learn that the period was very good for Roger Dexter's love life as well.

On the last Friday in every month there was a staff curry evening that everyone was invited to. The atmosphere was loud but light, if that's possible, and great friendships and a real fondness for the firm was formed.

Miss Bright missed out on four or five desperate dhansaks before going along herself, chaperoned by Lizzie from accounts, and two or three chicken bhoonas later she and Roger were actually conversing for the first time at the same table.

They talked about this and that but what really broke the ice was the fact that they were both big readers.

He stuck in the Brontes and George Eliot, for semi-tactical reasons, and she in turn skipped easily from Salinger to Solzhenitsyn.

Then came the clincher. Impossibly, they both loved Rex Stout. Rex bloody Stout.

'You've got to be kidding,' said Roger Dexter. 'I thought I was the only one.'

'No, not for a second, confound it!' said Verity Bright with Stoutian humour. 'And I have a confession to make.'

'What on earth could that be, not flummery surely?' asked Roger.

'Well,' said Verity, hesitating like one of Nero Wolfe's suspects in the brownstone. 'I think I've started to see something of Archie Goodwin in you.'

'Okay, yes, see. Understood,' said Roger in his best Archie voice. 'Things like this are bound to happen, see, when two souls like this collide.' Wolfe would have another phrase for it, I'm sure. But he'd certainly describe you as "comely".'

She smiled a lovely smile and things developed from there, as Archie would have predicted in the Nero Wolfe narrative.

That was three months ago and they're getting married next week. The reception is being held in the Curry Queen in Lewisham. Wolfe's comment? 'Pfui, Archie! What will Fritz think?'

Jamal's final appearance

THURSDAY evening's training went well despite the drizzle.

After the final 10 minutes of two-touch, which they all loved, 'coach' Tommy Bishop took striker Josh aside for five minutes of meeting the ball.

Josh was Lee United's top scorer but had been running offside in recent matches and Tommy was trying to get his first 'real movement' to be towards the ball instead of towards the goal.

"You can feint to go goalwards, Josh, in fact that's a great idea," said Tommy, demonstrating the feint on the spot despite his dodgy knees, "but always try and make your first move towards the ball."

The team-mate helping Josh in this mini-session was Jamal, the Rolls Royce in Lee United's midfield and the biggest young target of both the local pro clubs, a point or two apart in the middle of Division One, called that but in reality the third tier of English football.

Both sent scouts to check on Jamal's progress every Sunday morning.

These were Lee United's Under 12s, although most of the players had turned 12 by now. Most top 11/12-year-olds had already been snapped up – some having 'signed' for a pro club next to proud mums and dads at the age of seven or eight! – but Jamal was also very bright at school and his parents, his mum a doctor and dad a planning officer on the local council, didn't want him mixed up in all that hype just yet. Plus, their son loved playing for Lee United.

One of the scouts, dubbed Super Scout by all the mums and dads, chatted easily among them but always made sure he didn't leave the game without a quick word with Jamal's parents. His line was that Jamal was 'a bit special' but that the boy needed to play at a higher level at the pro club, against better players, to show how good he really was.

By the end of the five minutes' practice, Josh was getting the hang of it and Tommy was saying: "Terrific, Josh!" As they walked back to the dressing room, Tommy asked him: "Did that make sense, Josh? Did it feel better?"

"It did actually," said Josh. "Can we practice it every session?"

"Course we can," said Tommy. "There was a great professional coach years ago who talked about 'good habits' and that's all that meeting the ball is really, Josh, a good habit, like calling man on or turn."

Lee United were lying second in the A Division table, two points behind Eltham Rovers, who they would also meet in the League Cup Final on Sunday week. Everyone was very excited about that although Tommy and manager Barry Maggs tried to keep things as calm as possible.

Sunday's games would decide the league. Eltham Rovers were favourites but if they drew and Lee United won, Lee would take the title on goal difference.

Sunday came and Barry's pep talk in the dressing room followed the usual pattern: "Stick to your football, lads, pass and move, be brave, take a touch, you've usually got more time than you think, encourage each other, no moaning, no arguing with the ref – he's ALWAYS right! – and, most of all.."

"Enjoy YOURSELVES!" shouted the entire squad and Tommy Bishop.

At the start of the season, Barry and Tommy had got the parents together in the clubhouse – Lee United had two senior teams and five juniors, including the Under 12s. Barry did the no-nonsense talking: "Please don't be offended everyone but Tommy and I are asking you to be on your best behaviour on the touchline. Every match. We all know there has been trouble, even fights, between rival supporters at junior games, which we think is terrible and, frankly, we won't allow it at Lee United. So, if you don't mind, please leave the football to us and limit your support to encouragement only. All the variations between well done and bad luck are fine, but nothing more than that please."

One or two dads looked a bit taken aback, perhaps thinking they knew as much about football as Barry and Tommy, if not more, and fully expected to be able demonstrate that on the touchline. But Barry had made his point in no uncertain fashion. They could see he meant it.

On Sunday they were playing a mid-table side, Woolwich Youth, who had earned a reputation for being very hard to beat. They had no outstanding players but knew how to make life uncomfortable for the so-called stars they faced most Sunday mornings.

Their manager, Jimmy Gleeson, was a proper character with a smile for everyone, including referees, and non-stop encouragement for his team. Like Lee United, he also had a girl in his squad, a very fast mixed race girl called Charmaine, who played down the right. Lee's female was Evie, a defender whose block tackling came as a shock to boys who hadn't played against her before.

It was a good game, very close as expected. If anything Woolwich Youth had the edge for two thirds of the game. Goalkeeper Ginger Bates had to pull off two excellent saves and once again had a lot to say for himself and to his defenders.

It was only in the last 15 minutes that Lee United's skills started to show themselves. Josh put them in front – very close to being offside! – and his fellow striker, Kieran, made it 2-0 near the end. Jamal, as usual, looked different class, a point not missed by Super Scout.

The championship was theirs if Eltham Rovers lost or drew. The league leaders were playing a team, Kidbrooke Knights, who started the season well but had lost form since Christmas. Everyone at Lee United hoped they'd find it for just one more game.

Alas, that wasn't the case. Everyone had their own way of finding out the Eltham Rovers result. At least four players from each team went to the same secondary school – Year 7 – and would be texting each other with contrasting imojis!

Tommy knew Dave Johnson, the Eltham Rovers manager/coach, well – they played two seasons in the same team 15 years earlier. He called Dave and got the news, the bad news. Eltham Rovers won 3-0 and, in Dave's words, Kidbrooke Knights 'never really turned up'.

"Oh, well, well done Dave, they're really good lads, yours. They deserved it. You all deserved it over the season. We'll just have to win the cup!"

"Not if we can help it," laughed Dave. "Have a nervy week, Tommy!"

That's what it was, very nervy. Barry and Tommy stayed in the clubhouse for a drink and a chat after Tuesday training – they also trained on Thursdays – and decided, as usual, not to worry about the opponents they knew so well but only talk about their own players.

"Josh looked the perfect target man against Kidbrooke and Jamal looked better than ever," said Barry. "Did Super Scout have another word?"

"He did," said Tommy, "but Siddharth – 'one who has accomplished a goal', I looked it up! – and Suhani are great. Perhaps next season. We won't be able to hold him back for ever."

"Agreed, but it's not exactly the beautiful game in Division One any more, is it?"

"Where is it anywhere, mate? Winning ugly and 'taking one for the team' with a cynical tackle is how Sky Sports sees it, mate."

"Yeah but let's not get depressed. We've got a cup final coming up between two terrific teams and there won't be any diving. We know that."

"True. So what about the rest of the squad?"

"They're all in good form, I think, and the day won't phase them. I think we should get Nicola on at some point and we know that she and Evie will both be training with pro clubs' girls teams next season. How great is that?"

"Fantastic," said Tommy. "I also think every player should be on the pitch at some point or another, whatever the score. We don't want their cup final memory to be just cheering from the side."

"Agreed. Let's win beautiful. Extra encouragement for Billy as well, I think, That point you made in training about anticipation applied especially to him, I think – makes up for that slight lack of pace."

"And Ginger'll keep him at it. Great having a captain in goal. It'll be a great day, doing our best, doing Lee United proud, and..."

"Enjoying yourselves!" they both shouted with everyone in the bar looking their way.

They left the clubhouse, having got rid of their own nerves and being fully focused on the following Sunday. No injuries or sickness, thank goodness. No problems at all.

Except one...

Every junior team relies on volunteers and Lee United was no different. You need three or four parents to do three or four jobs and you nearly always find them, collecting subs, filling in the forms and paperwork for the league, buying and cutting the oranges.

Billy's mum, Sam, was an office worker who stepped in to do the players' registration forms, and it was great for Barry and Tommy, who both balked like hopeless schoolboys in those areas. Leave it to Sam and never give it a thought!

On the Friday evening Sam phoned Barry and sounded a bit worried. In fact she was worried, very worried.

"What's up, Sam? Don't tell me Billy's not well."

"Oh, no, no. Barry, you remember the league changed the qualifying birth dates of players at the end of last season? I couldn't go to the AGM, so you and Tommy filled in?"

"Yes," said Barry vaguely, feeling guilty already. "Not our forte, I'm afraid, Sam. Thank God we've got you most of the time. We just put our hands up every time everyone else did."

"Well, the upshot," said Sam, obviously upset, "was that Jamal was... too old for this season, by one day, from day one."

"What? Who's idea was that? Where did that come

from. Don't remember that. He was okay last season."

"I know," said Sam. "It was something from the FA to do with the start of the school year. Some bloody nonsense dreamed up by someone with nothing else to do. The way it worked out was that just two birth dates, one of them Jamal's, would be affected. If you had a player born on either of those two dates – I've got the minute in front of me now in black and white – you had to get special dispensation for this season and this season only."

"I don't even know what month Jamal was born," said Barry. "I just left all that in your capable hands. Tommy and I are hopeless. What can we do? Can we do anything?"

"Well," said Sam. "As things stand it looks like we are the only ones who know about it. Trust me to look through it all! I do a lot of checking in my job. To be honest, the league officials are unlikely to check, so we should get away with our guilty little secret."

"I'm sure we would," said Barry, "but what if someone finds out afterwards? Our name would be mud, and so would Lee United's, and I don't like the feel of it anyway."

"I think the same, Barry, but what about the team? What about Jamal? He won't understand because he qualified last season but not this, on a technicality. He'll be heartbroken, especially when he prefers Lee United to a professional club."

"Yes." Barry thought for a second and then said: "I'll tell you what, leave it with me, Sam, please, and I'll have a word with Tommy and let you know what's going to happen before Sunday. Okay? How's Billy, by the way?"

"So excited. He's grown so much in confidence since joining the team and even his school work has come on a lot. His dad and I love it as well."

As soon as he put the phone down, Barry called Tommy and put him in the picture. There was a few seconds silence before Tommy said anything. Then he said: "Barry, we can't keep this to ourselves. It woudn't be right"

"I know," said Barry. "I agree."

"I think the best thing we can do is tell Eltham Rovers, tell Dave Johnson and see what he thinks. We used to play together. He's a good lad."

"I know, but what will he be like if there's a chance of facing us without Jamal?"

"Mmm," said Tommy. "I know. Let's see."

Tommy called Dave, said something was up, and could they meet for a coffee in the morning. They met at Costa's in Eltham High Street, Rovers' territory.

Tommy bought the cappuccinos, Dave turned down a croissant, and was all ears as Tommy explained the sorry situation. At the end Dave just looked across the table at his old team-mate.

After a short pause, he grinned and said: "So what's the problem? There's no problem, mate. If Jamal doesn't play tomorrow I'll never speak to you again. I love the boy, love to watch him play. Now piss off!"

Tommy gulped and said he did indeed need a piss. He actually needed a few seconds to himself. He went to the toilet and looked himself in the eye in the mirror. It could indeed be a beautiful game.

Sunday came just like it did the week before. The final was played at a local semi-pro club's ground with a stand on one side of the pitch. The surface was like a billiard table and there must have been more than 500 spectators, including Super Scout and the local mayor who presented the trophy and medals.

Before he did that he gave a short speech saying that he had always loved his football and could hardly believe the incredible standard of play and sportsman-

ship he had just witnessed. 'Bravo!' he told the crowd.
Who won? Football did.

Winston's change of pace

WINSTON Brown doesn't like cricket, he loves it, but to this day, he tells me, he battles between the importance of sportsmanship and the fiery need to compete and win.

I just about make the same Sunday afternoon side. We've become good mates and have talked about his little attitude problem more than once. He reckons he's pretty much got it sorted but that the demons still pull his ears back and whisper into them from time to time..

Winston came to live in this country at the age of 17, 22 years ago. His mother and father are both doctors – one of them took the exam twice, according to Basil Fawlty – and he's now working himself in a caring profession, mainly with young people, in Bromley.

During our chats, I've often wondered if he could have made a career out of cricket, having been in the Guyana squad for a prestigious President's Cup match when still a teenager. Amazing really. But circumstances grabbed hold of his life the way they do with most of us.

Over here he married Priscilla and they now have two teenagers themselves, one of each, both lovely kids, Rachel and Brian – after Lara, I've always supposed. Winston and I play for our village team in Downe in Kent, and Brian, at 15, impressively makes up the numbers when needed.

It's not league cricket, just well-organised friendly Sunday afternoon matches that go back 50 years or more in that part of Kent. Winston's dichotomy between winning and losing didn't really show itself at this friendly level, but I always suspected that something might one day spark it.

And one day something did.

In Guyana, Winston was a fast bowler, and I mean fast. He was less Michael 'Whispering Death' Holding, more Curtly 'Crusher' Ambrose. But down Downe he decided to bowl medium pace or even the occasional gentle leg breaks and googlies out of the blue and out of the back of the hand.

He bats a bit as well and is still great in the field at extra cover. As a team, we win matches and lose matches, probably just a few more of the former.

Winston, at 39, is still in great shape, still resembling a middleweight boxer. He's much liked for his gentle smile and dry humour, but, without ever mentioning it amongst ourselves, everyone on match days makes a psychological decision not to rile him. Silly really but just one of those things people take upon themselves, like having a coffee with Tyson Fury and urging him to have just the one croissant.

Towards the end of Winston's first season in the team, there was some kind of chatter in the changing room about the following Sunday's opponents. 'Bloody Sevenoaks next week,' said Roger, wicket keeper and perennial No 11, 'and that bloody captain of theirs,

Superior Sidney, the bloke who played one match for Kent Seconds. Just one. Got me out the last three times and three times followed by that sickly grin under that shock of ginger hair.'

Our own captain, Nigel, from The City, told Roger not to keep on but just hit one of Sidney's leg breaks for six. The rest of us, including Winston, managed to change the subject to that day's game, me suggesting that Winston should leapfrog to No. 5 in the batting. The diverting chat did the trick, shutting Roger up. Once he gets going there's no stopping him.

We won that game by one wicket and, thank the lord, Roger hit the winning run, an edge to third man. But the match at Sevenoaks, as you're probably thinking, came soon enough. It was a lovely day, they laid on a super spread following our 176 all out, yours truly making what captain Nigel called a stylish 22.

However, Superior Sidney had got Roger out yet again, our man failing to spot the slower ball yet again. Followed, of course – yet again - by the Sidney grin. But this time it had got worse. Roger had lost it and called Superior Sidney a name that wasn't cricket. Two or three of us had to step in to prevent Roger attacking the sneering bowler.

I'd like to add that it ruined the tea and scones, but nothing could have. The Sevenoaks ladies were superb and we just made sure that Roger and Sidney sat at opposite ends of the long table shared amicably enough by the two teams.

Everyone who plays team sports knows that these things happen, and there's not really anything anyone can do about it. You just have to keep it as calm as can be, shake as many hands as possible and avoid bloodshed on the decking. Otherwise you get yourself a name and end up losing fixtures.

That's why we were all ready to make peace at Sevenoaks on that late August afternoon with cows mooing and smiling to themselves in the adjacent field. But we didn't know that something else was stirring in the breast of one cricketer as the church bell chimed half past six.

Sevenoaks, always a strong batting side, reached 173 for 5 at the start of the last over bowled by Winston Brown. By the fifth ball the scores were level and Superior Sidney – who else? – turned on the grin as Nigel, at mid-on as usual, lobbed the ball to Winston for the last ball of the day.

Roger, hallucinating by now behind the stumps, seemed to see or feel someone jump very suddenly to his immediate right. It was no one, of course. He was just beside himself. Then he crouched down behind the stumps, hoping against hope that somehow Sidney wouldn't be able to hit the winning run off the very last ball. The latter was a good batsman and a lethally quick runner. A simple single looked a certainty. Not a bye, please not a bye, Roger prayed to himself.

Roger was ready and so was Sidney but, strangely, Winston wasn't. Winston just stood there next to the umpire and the batsman at the bowler's end. They both looked at him. Roger looked at him. Even Sidney, without grinning, looked at him. Nigel wondered what was going on. 'Play,' said the umpire, trying to move things on and thinking about his first pint at The Chequers. But still Winston just stood there, seemingly meditating.

Then he did something we hadn't seen before. He motioned Roger to move back from the stumps. Roger didn't understand but walked backwards a few feet. Winston kept motioning with both hands until Roger was fully 20 yards from the stumps and a now befuddled Superior Sidney. By this time everyone at the ground were exchanging bewildered looks. Even the cows stood there wondering.

Then Winston, instead of retreating a couple of steps as usual, went back 20 yards himself, turned and roared in like Curtley Ambrose at the Providence Stadium, Guyana, and pitched it short.

He was also the first to send the pole-axed Sidney a Get Well Soon card. Match tied.

The local sprinter

SHE was a sprinter aged 14 or 15, better at 220 than 100 as I recall her telling me in the café at the neat little track in Lee. But it was what she achieved off the track around that time that made her so special and, at the same time, got my own career off the ground.

I was only 18 myself and the cub reporter at the local paper, the Chronicle. But I wasn't very good at it, to be honest, stuck somewhere between hopeless and hapless, a working class boy struggling in a middle class world.

It was only the kind old editor, Charlie King, who kept me on after the obligatory six-month trial. If it had been left to the grumpy chief sub – whose journalistic rewards included an annual bottle of whisky from the local Conservative Association – I would have been told where the door was.

My one ray of hope was sport. I was a promising footballer and cricketer myself at that time and felt I could report on local sport. The sports editor – a pipe-smoking character called Harold Deacon – obviously held similar hopes, knowing that I played a bit.

He got me started on the bowls and darts results before calling me into his tiny office one Friday morning.

'Jimmy,' he said, 'I want you to go to Sutcliffe Park on Sunday morning and cover the Kent Athletics League meeting. Cambridge Harriers are the home team and I want you to interview two or three of their best competitors, obviously if they win races or one of the field events. Bev will be taking the pictures so liaise with her, okay?'

I said okay and got up to leave. 'Oh, and one more thing,' said Harold. 'Ask them how they got into athletics in the first place. Sometimes you find out more about them that way. It might even lead to a separate, human interest story on a news page. You never know.'

I nodded without really getting the point. You've probably worked out already that I didn't really have a nose for news. So I just went down to see Beverley in the photographers' retreat – there were three of them in those good old days – and arranged to meet her at Sutcliffe Park on the Sunday morning. She was mid-thirties and, like most of the others in the newsroom, I could tell she was not over-impressed by the latest cub reporter.

Sunday came and I got there early. Beverley knew from previous experience that the big races and field events came much later, so I bought myself a coffee and croissant to watch the more junior races. It was the first time that I could actually picture myself as a fully-fledged sports reporter, given the skills and loads more experience.

What impressed me straight away was how commitment seemed to come so easily to all the competitors, the way they walked and talked and were ready to give it their all. The atmosphere was terrific and I decided to practice my interviewing techniques before the big races later on and before Beverley was anywhere within hearing distance.

The next race was the 100 metres for Under 16 girls and the sprinter I'm telling you about was in lane three. Her name was Teresa Brown – not Green! – and she finished second after a slight stumble at the start. As she and a team-mate walked past me to the Cambridge Harriers tent, I noticed what a bubbly character she was, chatting away non-stop to her team mates.

I remembered what Harold Deacon had said to me about asking competitors how they got into athletics in the first place, so I waited for Teresa Brown to head my way about 10 minutes later. I was suddenly attacked by self-consciousness but managed to say: 'Sorry, excuse me, I'm from the Chronicle and would like to interview you if you don't mind.'

She gave me a massive big smile and said: 'Yeah, of course, but I only finished second.'

'I know,' I said, 'but our sports editor asked me to ask people how they got into athletics in the first place.' I'm surprised that in my nervousness I didn't give the address of the Gazette in Wellington Street and how the weekly paper came out once a week.

She smiled again and calmed me down. 'Well,' she said, 'it's nothing special. I came here two years ago with my friend here, Janey, and just got to enjoy it. It was pretty obvious early on that I would never make the Olympics but it's all very enjoyable.

'We compete every Sunday and Janey's dad drives us to away league matches as far as Maidstone, so it's quite something. I'm thinking of trying the long jump to help the team out because we need to cover as many events as possible and get extra points.'

I was taking it all down with a Dictaphone, shorthand being another of the journalistic skills I was struggling with. I thought I had enough from Teresa to go with quotes from the older competitors later on, but then came a question from Janey that went on to change my life.

'Ask her about the foodbank,' grinned Janey.

'Foodbank?' I said.

Teresa Brown clearly didn't want to go there but, with Janey's help over the next 10 minutes, I got the whole story. It turned out that Teresa the sprinter also 'ran' a fortnightly foodbank from the conservatory at her home in nearby Kidbrooke.

With help from friends and family, she bought food and necessities from Lidl or Aldi. The family followed that up by arranging with a drop-in club for the homeless in Deptford to make a spare room available for victims of domestic violence whenever it was needed.

My report was greatly improved by Charlie King's experienced 'sub editing' and Beverley's brilliant pictures. It got Teresa and my byline on the front page the following Thursday, with the grumpy chief sub's admittedly excellent headline: 'Saint Teresa!'

2084

IT'S 2084 and somehow the world is a much better place.

Take Jennifer. Jenny. She turned 60 last week and followed up her Freemail by catching a free taxi to the town hall.

At the desk she said she'd come to see Mr Jones in the Special Gifts and Donations Department. The old man behind the desk smiled. He had a patch over where his left had been.

'Ooh,' said Jenny. 'Did you give an eye?'

'Yes,' said the man. The nametag in front of him said Mr Jones. He smiled again: 'I like to call it an eye for an eye. What about you?'

'Oh, just a kidney,' said Jennifer, 'the same as most people.' She smiled at the smiling man and headed for the lifts after being told third floor.

The idea will be ten years old next year. Some reckon it's the most wonderful initiative there's ever been on Earth. The take up has been amazing all over the planet.

When people get to 60 in this new world they can/ are encouraged to give a Special Gift to a fellow human being who needs it. As Jenny told the man, a kidney is the easiest and most popular gift, one kidney being enough for all of us.

The Poverty Gap no longer exists in the TUK (Truly United Kingdom) and there are no wars taking place anywhere, thank God. Progress has been fantastic and newspapers and television have been full of it for 25 years or more, telling the good news instead of choosing to sell mainly misery.

There's no homelessness and everyone, literally everyone in this country, helps her/his global neighbour every day of the week in one way or another. We have not only given peace a chance, it's taken over the place.

There's no greed. No pride. No jealousy to speak of. No hankerings for money or power or position.

In the Pre Times, as we all call them, there were some who thought that life would be intolerably boring without ambition and competition, that Utopia was not only impossible but unwanted. Nowadays everyone realises that it was not only possible, it was perfectly natural and normal.

We still have sports and all sorts of competitions, but taking defeat badly – 'taking one for the team,' for example – would be ridiculous, laughable. We all share victory. Victory is not only winning but sharing the experience. The winning at all costs mentality belongs with the dinosaurs.

Jenny got out at the third floor and went along the corridor to a huge room marked New Gifts. As she entered the room there was spontaneous applause from about 100 people with spaces for 50 more. Jenny was taken aback before she moved forward into the throng.

'You must be Jennifer,' said Mr Ali. She didn't

know how he could have known, she hadn't sent a photograph or anything, but she just accepted it. Acceptance had become one of the keys by 2084.

The atmosphere in the room struck her as something special. Her antennae as a young woman, years earlier, would have perked up and sensed some kind of scam, but those days and experiences are long gone.

'Kidney?' said Mr Ali.

'Yes, please,' said Jenny, 'if that's okay/'

'Of course, of course,' said Mr Ali. 'First, if you don't mind, I'd like to give a brief history of Special Gifts and the circumstances – the individual – that gave rise to them. The general idea is that most people, certainly more than was thought possible 100 years ago, feel like making a wonderful contribution – a Special Gift – by the time they reach the age of 60, a nice round number.

'Now that the world is more peaceful and caring than it's ever been, the number of people wanting to make a Special Gift is quite extraordinary. The evidence is here today. It's like this every day.

Jenny looked around the huge room and nodded to Mr Johnson. It was something she could have never imagined as a little girl 50 years earlier.

'Are you allowed to tell me about the brilliant man who had the idea in the first place, Mr Ali? There are so many different stories.'

'Yes, I am,' he said, 'but it's best not to spread too many details because it's so important for the great changes in the world to speak for themselves. The man involved went missing, disappeared for a long, long time, but then suddenly returned.'

'Wow,' said Jennifer, 'and what a difference he has made. Have you ever met him, Mr Ali?'

'Oh yes, many times,' said Mr Ali. 'It's very easy to meet him. He's been here many times. You just have to think about him really.'

'Just think about him, really?' repeated Jennifer.

'Oh, yes,' said Mr Ali. 'In fact, if you close your eyes tightly, concentrate for a just a few seconds and then open them again, you'll see him across the room today. I guarantee it.'

'Wow!' said Jennifer. She closed her eyes tightly, only for a few seconds, then opened them and looked across the room, first to the left and then to the right. A bearded man in a white top was talking quietly to a small group of people, who were clearly enrapt.

'Jesus!' exclaimed Jenny.

98

About the author

PETER CORDWELL was born in a Catford prefab in November, 1947. He passed the 11-plus at nearby Forster Park primary school but domeheads at Brockley County Grammar School (now defunct) turned him down after hearing that his Dad was a driver and his Mum a homehelp.

He was a journalist for more than 50 years, starting at the Kentish Independent in Woolwich and eventually becoming sports editor/editor of the SE London Mercury and Greenwich Time, Greenwich Council's newspaper nicknamed 'Pravda' (and that's another story). He received two UK press awards, the second for the fans' campaign to get Charlton Athletic back to their home at The Valley.

He also played two seasons for VPS (Vaasan Palloseura) in the Finnish premier division (1975/76) and wrote the proletarian George Orwell musical/cabaret One Georgie Orwell with Charlton singer-songwriter Carl Picton.

Printed in Great Britain
by Amazon